"This is a must-read book, not just because the authors have great insight to share on the topic, but because this is the most needed book for all Christians today. Many Christians believe the future of Christianity is the virtual church, and COVID-19 is reinforcing this idea. You will find *Rediscover Church* very helpful as a reminder to firmly stand on the biblical view of the church and nothing else. I cannot recommend this book highly enough."

Nima Alizadeh, President and Founder, Iranian Revelation Ministries Inc.

"This is a very timely book in an age of confusion and disappointment regarding the essential need of the local church. Hansen and Leeman have provided a logical, practical, biblical, and basic understanding of the role of the church in the life of a believer. It is hard to imagine a Christian who is maturing in Christ and living the gospel consistently apart from a local church. If you wonder why that is, you need to read this book to be convinced and encouraged. I hope and pray that our God will use this book to contribute to the rediscovery and rebuilding of the church in our days."

Miguel Núñez, Senior Pastor, International Baptist Church of Santo Domingo, Dominican Republic

"Even before the COVID-19 pandemic, widely different views on the Christian church had emerged. The restrictions due to the pandemic have further challenged our view on what the church and its function is; a biblical recovery is therefore needed more than ever. Collin Hansen and Jonathan Leeman have risen to this challenge and offer this book to help us toward such a recovery. Written in a lucid, conversational style, *Rediscover Church* offers a compelling, biblical view full of insight and practical wisdom. It should be read and discussed in every church because it offers important biblical guidance to help believers rediscover the church of Jesus Christ for his glory and for the progress of the gospel."

Kees van Kralingen, Elder, Independent Baptist Church of Papendrecht, The Netherlands; Editor, *Reformation Today*; Council Member, The Gospel Coalition Nederland

"*Rediscover Church* is a timely, relevant book sorely needed for the post-pandemic world. No longer can church be taken for granted; this generation wants to know why we're doing what we're doing. Hansen and Leeman deftly combine biblical thought with real-world experience to deliver a manifesto of what the church should be today. Why do we physically gather in a virtual world? Who has given the church authority to proclaim truth? How do we love those inside and outside the church? How do we practice the tough love of church discipline? At times hard-hitting (the immorality of homogeneous churches), chock-full of memorable illustrations (the church as an embassy), and always thoughtful, this is a book your church should be reading and talking about."

J. Mack Stiles, missionary and former pastor in the Middle East; author, *Evangelism*

"Once upon a time, the basic truths about the church were foreign only to nominal Christians who had abandoned church commitment long ago. With the entry of COVID-19 and the availability of live-streaming services, more and more believers are preferring to 'do church' at home. Therefore, this easy-to-read book, rich with personal anecdotes, has come out at a crucial time. Collin Hansen and Jonathan Leeman invite us to rediscover church by savoring one all-embracing definition of the church. Walking with them through this book will give you a renewed love for the church and its head, the Lord Jesus Christ."

Conrad Mbewe, Pastor, Kabwata Baptist Church, Lusaka, Zambia

Rediscover Church

Rediscover Church

Why the Body of Christ Is Essential

Collin Hansen
and Jonathan Leeman

WHEATON, ILLINOIS

Cover image & design: Crystal Courtney

First printing, 2021

Printed in the United States of America

Trade paperback ISBN: 978-1-4335-7956-1

ePub ISBN: 978-1-4335-7959-2

PDF ISBN: 978-1-4335-7957-8

Mobipocket ISBN: 978-1-4335-7958-5

Library of Congress Cataloging-in-Publication Data

Names: Hansen, Collin, 1981– author. | Leeman, Jonathan, 1973– author.

Title: Rediscover church: why the body of Christ is essential / Collin Hansen and Jonathan Leeman.

Description: Wheaton, Illinois: Crossway, 2021. | Series: 9Marks and the gospel coalition | Includes index.

Identifiers: LCCN 2021005473 (print) | LCCN 2021005474 (ebook) | ISBN 9781433579561 (trade paperback) | ISBN 9781433579578 (pdf) | ISBN 9781433579585 (mobi) | ISBN 9781433579592 (epub)

Subjects: LCSH: Church.

Classification: LCC BV600.3 .H437 2021 (print) | LCC BV600.3 (ebook) | DDC 262/.7—dc23

LC record available at https://lccn.loc.gov/2021005473

LC ebook record available at https://lccn.loc.gov/2021005474

Crossway is a publishing ministry of Good News Publishers.

BP		29	28	27	26	25	24	23	22	21
14	13	12	11	10	9	8	7	6	5	4	3	2	1

For my home group:
Those who pandemic together, stay together

Collin

To my brothers and sisters at Cheverly Baptist Church

Jonathan

Contents

Introduction

YOU MAY HAVE MANY reasons not to go to church. Indeed, many people stopped attending during the recent pandemic—as much as one-third of churchgoers by some estimates. You may be one of them. But this book aims to help you rediscover church. Or maybe it can help you discover for the first time why God wants you to make a priority of gathering with and committing yourself to the local church.

Simply put, a Christian without a church is a Christian in trouble.

We're long past the time when we could assume even that dedicated believers in Jesus Christ understood why they should bother with church. The number who identify as Christians is far larger than the number who attend a weekly meeting. Even then, the bulk of the serving and giving in our churches tends to be done by only a few. So it's not as if COVID-19 suddenly convinced Christians they didn't need church. Millions had already made that decision even before gathering involved online registration, social distancing, and masks.

COVID-19, however, accelerated the long-trending separation between personal faith and organized religion. The shutdowns caught all of us by surprise in their sudden onset and indefinite duration. And it's hard to get back in the habit once it's been broken for more than a year. That problem is not unique to church. Try getting back to the gym when you've been scared to darken the doors for months.

Resuming church attendance would be hard enough if our only problem were that a deadly disease kept us apart much longer than many expected. But fear of contracting COVID-19 might be the least of the reasons that convinced many Christians to stay away from church. Debates over masks, vaccines, and much else divided church members trapped in their homes and glued to Facebook feeds filled with dire warnings and conspiracy theories. Christians liked each other a lot more before social media. Take away the unifying experience of weekly worship together under the same roof, and the bonds of affection have frayed.

But that's not all. Recent elections—for American readers, at least—might have been even more divisive. How can Christians worship alongside voters with such different priorities? Sure, Christians might share the same views on the Trinity, baptism, and even eschatology. But what good is that when we feel more in common with our political allies who might not even be Christians?

The same goes for the causes of racial unrest. Why can unbelieving neighbors see the solutions so clearly, we might wonder, when the couple we used to sit behind at church every week promotes such ignorant and even dangerous views in their public postings? It's enough to make many think they could never be safe or comfortable returning to that same church.

And don't ask about pastors. They've heard our complaints. Why didn't they reach out to check on us while we were locked down at home? How did they even spend their time during the pandemic? The online sermons were lackluster, when anyone bothered to tune in while distracted by stir-crazy children. Anyway, regular pastors can't compare to the courageous leaders who tackled the issues head-on in TV interviews and articles. Plus, the pandemic made it easier than ever before to watch other pastors' online sermons without guilt and skip our own church. We knew that no one would ever know the difference, since we couldn't see our pastors in person anyway.

Yes, we all have many reasons not to go back to church. In fact, many churches don't expect us to ever come back. They're launching virtual churches and hiring virtual pastors. No need to wake up early on Sunday. No need to put on pants. No need to search for a parking spot. No need to tune out other people's crying babies. No need to make small talk over bad coffee with the person whose politics disgusts you. No need to stifle a yawn through a long sermon. No need to taste the bread and the wine.

A Future for the Church?

Is there a future, then, for church? Is virtual church the future? Yes and no. That's why we aim in this book to convince you to rediscover church. We don't do so from naivete, as if we can't imagine why someone would struggle with the local church. In fact, anyone who loves the church must learn to forgive and forbear with Christians. God does not invite us to church because it's a comfortable place to find a bit of spiritual encouragement. No, he invites us into a spiritual family of misfits and outcasts. He welcomes us into a home that's rarely what we want yet just what we need.

Try to remember church before the pandemic. When you looked around the congregation gathered to sing, pray, and hear God's Word, you might have thought everyone was happy to be there. They might have listened quietly as the pastor preached or shouted "Amen!" when they wanted to affirm a point. They might have raised their hands as the choir led in song or buried their eyes in a hymnal. They might have extended a warm handshake and a friendly hello or offered a quick "Peace be with you" before moving on.

But not everything is as it seems, even in a church full of smiles. The pandemic strained our relationships and surfaced some of the pain and fear behind the happy faces.

Behind every smile in church you'll find a story. You'll find a family that bickered all the way from home until they crossed the building threshold. You'll find a widow grieving a loss that everyone else has already forgotten. You'll find a solitary soul wrestling with doubt about God's goodness amid a lifetime of pain and suffering. You might even find a pastor wondering how he can plead with the church to follow Jesus after a week when he so often has failed to do so himself.

From week to week in your church, you can never be quite sure how everyone feels or what everyone thinks, no matter their appearance. You can't even be quite sure why everyone shows up. That's why you don't know who will come back. One person thoroughly researched various churches' doctrinal positions before selecting the best match. Another person just needed friends in a new town. One person has bounced from congregation to congregation and never found the right fit. Another person can't imagine any reason to leave the church where she grew up and observed every milestone of birth, marriage, and death. By appearance alone, you never can tell the full story, even in your own church.

So why would you rediscover church? What could get you out of bed again on a Sunday morning or off the couch after work on a Wednesday night? Why would you return to a particular congregation among other options? Why even bother with Christianity at all? The world hardly mourned the absence of church during the pandemic. What is it, anyway? Is it a self-help club for the mentally and emotionally weak? Is it a political action group for the like- and closed-minded? Is it a community-service organization for people who enjoy old-timey songs?

Even before the threat of deadly contagion, the church looked increasingly strange in an age when neighbors rarely gather for things like intimate discussion, quiet learning, and enthusiastic singing—especially when the subject matter comes from an ancient book about strange practices such as animal sacrifice, a book that Christians regard as having absolute authority.

What exactly happens, then, when you go to church? We don't just mean things like the sermon, the singing, and the service (though we'll address all those things and more in this little book). We're talking about what happens beyond the smiles, beyond the songs, beyond the Scripture reading. We're talking about the plans and purposes of God—because your church is much more than meets the eye. It is, in fact, the apple of God's eye, the body for which Jesus Christ gave his body. It's essential.

That's why God uses the most intimate of human relationships, marriage, to explain what's happening in your church. Teaching the church in Ephesus about marriage, the apostle Paul writes:

Husbands, love your wives, as Christ loved the church and gave himself up for her, that he might sanctify her, having cleansed her by the washing of water with the word, so that he might present the church to himself in splendor, without spot or wrinkle or any such thing, that she might be holy and without blemish. (Eph. 5:25–27)

In this passage, Paul helps us deduce from a relationship we know, marriage, in order to understand something about the church that we cannot see. Husbands love their wives by giving up their lives. Likewise, Jesus Christ—God's only Son, conceived by the Holy Spirit, born of the virgin Mary, crucified by order of Rome, risen from the dead on the third day—gave himself up for the church. Through his sacrifice on the cross, he pardoned all who turn from their sin and trust him. You can be holy because Jesus gave his body. Just as you nourish and cherish your body, so Christ nourishes and cherishes his church (Eph. 5:29).

Imagine the profound mystery of Christ and the church when the old lady next to you wears too much perfume, when the guy in front of you claps on the wrong beats, and when your friend on the other end of the aisle forgets to tell you "Happy birthday!" It's even harder to imagine that mystery when you're home alone, because even and especially the awkward members of the body remind us that no one approaches God except by sheer grace. No one can buy a seat at this table. You can only be invited.

Believe it or not, your church gets even more interesting. The apostle Paul tells the church in Corinth, "Now you are the body of Christ and individually members of it" (1 Cor. 12:27). Yes, your church is the very body of Christ. That goes for the banker who chairs your deacon board and the recovering alcoholic who can't control his body odor. That goes for the homecoming queen who greets you with a smile at the door and the nursery worker who has never been on a date. If you have repented of sin and believed the good news of Jesus's death and resurrection, you all belong to Christ—and one another. Paul tells the Romans, "For as in one body we have many members, and the members do not all have the same function, so we, though many, are one body in Christ, and individually members one of another" (Rom. 12:4–5).

In Christ, your church is perfect—without spot or wrinkle. That holds true even in a pandemic and through political turmoil. In practice, you already know—or you'll eventually find out—that your church comprises members who still sin against God and one another even as the Spirit sanctifies them. They step on your toes. They forget to show up for child-care duty. They say offensive things. They demonstrate sinful partiality. And the list goes on.

But as we help you rediscover church in this book, you'll need to remind yourself of what you cannot see. You return to church because you belong to God, because Christ gave his body. And because he gave his body, Christ made a body of believers from every tribe, language, people, and nation (Rev. 5:9). In this body, no one person is more important than any other, because everyone belongs by grace alone through faith alone. There is no partiality for the rich, no preference for the important (James 2:1–7). Because we owe all to Christ, we share all with one another: "If one member suffers, all suffer together; if one member is honored, all rejoice together" (1 Cor. 12:26).

You belong to God and to one another. One body, many members—including you. You have many reasons not to rediscover church and one reason why you must: because through these people you don't much like, God wants to show his love to you. It's the only kind of love that can draw us out of ourselves and into a fellowship that transcends the forces tearing apart our sick world. It's the only essential way for us to find healing together.

Beyond all that, your church is where Christ says he's present in a unique way. We would even dare to say that your church and ours is where heaven touches down on earth—where our prayers begin to be answered: "Your kingdom come, your will be done, on earth as it is in heaven."

1

What Is a Church?

Jonathan Leeman

MAYBE YOUR PARENTS took you to church as a child. Mine did. Some things I liked. Others I didn't. One thing I loved was playing hide-and-seek with my friends in the church building. It was a sprawling, irregular building, with unexpected hallways, doorways, and stairwells—perfect for hide-and-seek. If you had asked me, "What is a church?" I probably would have pointed to the building.

In high school, the main thing that interested me about church was the Friday night youth events with fun songs, silly skits, and a quick devotion. But if you had asked me whether I had ever considered joining the actual church, I would not have known what to say. Probably I would have waved away the question, not seeing its relevance.

In college and graduate school, I stopped attending church. I still believed the truths of Christianity, at least in my head. Yet

I wanted the world more than I wanted Jesus. So I pursued the world with gusto. As best I can tell, I was a nominal Christian—a Christian in name only. I called Jesus my Savior, but he certainly wasn't my Lord. I "believed," but I hadn't "repented and believed," as Jesus calls us to do. Had you asked me, "What is a church?" I probably would have said, "It's a bunch of people who want to follow Jesus, which is why I don't want to be there." Ironically, the further I had strayed from the church, the better I had understood what it is.

What about you? Have you ever stopped and asked yourself, "What is a church?"

Preaching and People

In August 1996, I completed graduate school and moved to Washington, DC, to find a job. A Christian friend told me about a church in town. Feeling a little guilty about how I was living, but mostly desiring something deeper and more meaningful out of life, I decided to attend. I don't remember the sermon that first Sunday morning back at church, but I remember returning that night for the Sunday evening service and also the following Wednesday evening for Bible study. The following week, I attended the same: Sunday morning, Sunday night, then Wednesday night. I suddenly transformed from a nonattender to a three-times-a-week attender. Nobody made me. Something was drawing me.

Actually, *someone* was drawing me—the Holy Spirit—and he was using two things. First, he used Pastor Mark's preaching. I had never heard anything like it. Mark preached the Bible verse by verse, chapter by chapter, without embarrassment.

For instance, one Sunday Mark preached one of those difficult-to-stomach chapters in the Old Testament book of Joshua. God commanded Joshua to enter a Canaanite city and kill every man and woman, young and old, as well as all the cattle, sheep, and donkeys. He read the text out loud, looked up at us, and paused.

What is he going to say next, I wondered. *That text is outrageous!*

Finally, Pastor Mark spoke: "If you are a Christian, you should know why a text like that is in the Bible."

Wait, what?

At first, I was annoyed by Mark's challenge. *I should know why it's in the Bible? Why don't you tell me why it's in the Bible, Mr. Preacher!*

Yet a moment later, Mark's challenge started making sense. Verses like the one Mark had read remind us that God doesn't owe us explanations. We owe him explanations. God is not on trial. We are on trial. He is the Creator and Judge. Only he can give life and can take life.

I don't remember what Pastor Mark said next. The point is, my world had already changed. Reality had been reordered. I was seeing with a slightly different set of eyes—kind of like the new perspectives one acquires with age, but gained in an instant. A conviction had settled in: *God is God. I am not.*

Good preaching does this kind of work every week. It faithfully reveals the Bible and changes the eyes of your heart, helping you see the world from God's perspective, not your own. We'll think more about preaching in chapter 4.

Yet preaching like this wasn't the only thing the Holy Spirit used to draw me into that church. He also used the people. A man named Dan invited me to join his family every Saturday morning for breakfast and a study of Isaiah. A retired couple named Helen and Hardin invited me for dinner. So did another older couple named Paul and Alice. The church's embrace was sweet and warm. I had a few non-Christian college friends there in DC with me, yet more and more I wanted to spend time with these new church friends as well, and to invite my college friends to join us.

This congregation, its loves and commitments, offered me a picture of a different kind of life. I had lived to serve myself. They lived to serve God and others. I used my words to show off or to criticize. They used their words to encourage. I talked about God as if he was a chapter of philosophy. They talked about God as if they knew him. I wanted to enjoy the weekend party. They wanted to enjoy Christ.

The congregation also gave me a picture of a different kind of city. There we were in Washington, DC, a city awhirl in conversation about the upcoming elections of November 1996. Members, too, enjoyed such conversations. Some of them even departed to home districts for several weeks of campaigning for their bosses' congressional or senatorial seats. Yet these folks talked about politics as if it was merely *important*. The city wanted them to treat it as *ultimate*. Church members had political *interest*. The city wanted us to worship politics as an *idol*.

That meant that inside the church, the political culture felt . . . calmer, not frenzied, more respectful. Our agreement over truly ultimate things, like the source of eternal justice, allowed us to disagree lovingly over important things, like the best political strategies for justice now.

Traditional demographic divides also held less sway. I was a single man in my early twenties. With time, I spent more and more evenings with married couples in their seventies or a widow in her eighties. My first meaningful and deep friendships with minority brothers and sisters would occur in that church.

In short, I learned that the city of God marches to a different drummer even as it participates in some of the civic and cultural marches in the cities of this world.

If you had asked me in those days, "What is a church?" I could not have given you a well-formed answer. But these two ideas of preaching and people—a gospel word and a gospel society—were growing in prominence in my mind. A church—I knew—has something to do with a group of people gathering to be shaped by God's Word. That way, they begin to live together as a different kind of people, one that's both *in* and *not of* the world.

Why a Right Understanding Matters—Living Like Heaven

Let's bring it back to you again: What would you say a church is?

When we don't think about that question carefully, we risk cheating ourselves out of the sweet goodness that God intends for us through his family. After all, your *understanding* of what the church is will shape your *life* and your *living*.

For instance, think about how people today talk about "joining" a church, as if it's a club. Or "driving down to the church," as if it's a building. Or "enjoying church," as if it's a show. What assumptions are at work when we talk about church in these ways? Further, how do these assumptions shape how we engage with our churches? I'd say they make it easy to think about our churches for ninety minutes a week and ignore them otherwise.

"But hold on," we hear from the Scriptures. "A church is actually a gathering and a fellowship of the family of God, the body of Christ, and the temple of the Spirit." So if we continue to mindlessly treat our churches as little more than clubs, buildings, or performances, we'll miss the truckload of support and blessing that God means to park in our driveways.

This book aims to help you rediscover church so that you both *understand* what a church is and in turn discover the richness of *living* as a brother or sister in the family of God; the joy of *living* as one part of Christ's body united to other parts of the body; and the countercultural power of *living* as one brick in the holy temple where God dwells on earth now. We want you to experience all these benefits and blessings, both for your own sake and for the sake of your non-Christian friends and neighbors.

More than anything else, your non-Christian friends need not just your gospel words but also a gospel community that testifies to the truth of those gospel words. You want them to watch the life of your church and say, "God really does change people. And he really is building a just and righteous city—here in the church" (see 1 Cor. 14:25; Heb. 11:10).

Just think: American political leaders have long referred to America as a "city on a hill." Yet part of rediscovering church is rediscovering that *our churches* should be those cities on the hill, whether we live in the United States or any other nation. This is what we all—Christian and non-Christian—most need in culturally and politically tumultuous times.

Heaven will not descend to earth through any nation today. And it hasn't descended to earth among any nation since God tied his presence to the temple of ancient Israel.

Yet remarkably, amazingly, astoundingly, your church, the one we want you to rediscover, is the place where the Bible says heaven has begun to descend to earth:

- The kingdom of heaven is at hand here (Matt. 4).
- God's will is done on earth as it is in heaven here (Matt. 6).
- We store up the treasures of heaven here (Matt. 6).
- We bind and loose on earth what's bound and loosed in heaven here (Matt. 16, 18).
- We are the heavenly temple (1 Cor. 3; 1 Pet. 2).

Heaven touches down on planet earth through our gathered churches. And when this happens, you offer the citizens of your nation the hope of a better nation, the residents of your city the hope of a better and lasting city.

No matter what challenges you face as an American or non-American, ethnic minority or majority, rich or poor, your hope for a just and peaceful society should not rest on the kingdoms of this world. It should rest on the King himself, who is establishing his heavenly kingdom in the outposts we call the local church.

What Is a Church?

What is a church? The Bible uses all kinds of metaphors to answer that question—the family and household of God, the body of Christ, the temple of the Spirt, the pillar and foundation of truth, the bride of Christ, Christ's flock, and more. Each one of those metaphors tells us something wonderful about your church and ours. We need all of those metaphors because there is no other organization, body, or people like the church. We discussed a couple in the introduction, and we'll continue to mention them throughout this book.

Yet here's the theological definition of a church that we'll spend the rest of the book unpacking:

A church is a group of Christians (chapter 2)

↓

who assemble as an earthly embassy of
Christ's heavenly kingdom (chapter 3)

↓

to proclaim the good news and
commands of Christ the King (chapter 4);

↓

to affirm one another as his citizens
through the ordinances (chapter 5);

↓

and to display God's own
holiness and love (chapter 6)

↓

through a unified and
diverse people (chapter 7)

↓

in all the world (chapter 8),

↓

following the teaching and
example of elders (chapter 9).

Finally, a Member

A couple months after I arrived in DC, one of my new friends invited me to join the church. Actually, he invited me to move into the church's men's house, yet only church members were permitted to live in the house. It was a nice row house on Capitol Hill—a desirable neighborhood—and the rent was cheap. "Sure, I'll join the church! Tell me how to sign up," I said.

What I intended for financial gain, God intended for my good.

The church asked me to sit through several membership classes and an interview with Pastor Mark before joining. Having grown up in church, I knew the right answers. The congregation then voted to receive me as a member in November 1996.

If you had asked me at that time what a church is, I assume my answer would have been vague and generic. I do remember walking back from lunch one day with Pastor Mark and giving him a hard time about why our church insisted on being "Baptist." Those were the kinds of fights twenty-three-year-old me would pick.

Truth be told, I had one foot in and one foot out for the first year. On Saturday night, I partied with non-Christian friends. On Sunday morning, I went to church. It was like trying to stand on two horses at once. You know that won't last long.

But the Lord was gracious. Little by little, he changed my desires, and I began to place both feet on one horse. I began to repent and look to Jesus as both Savior and Lord. The Bible became interesting. Christian friends became precious. Sin increasingly seemed stupid, even detestable.

Repentance included abandoning the sins of my youth—the kind that youth pastors warn high schoolers about.

Yet biblical repentance also has a corporate dimension. In my case, it meant abandoning my life as an unattached, autonomous individual. It meant joining a family and taking responsibility for that family. It meant inviting other Christians into my life and having embarrassing conversations that included confessing sin or admitting weakness. It involved looking for older men to disciple me and younger men to disciple. It led me to show hospitality to folks who were new or in need. It trained me to rejoice or suffer with those who rejoice or suffer.

To put it another way, repentance always involves love. Jesus said, "A new commandment I give to you, that you love one another: just as I have loved you, you also are to love one another. By this all people will know that you are my disciples, if you have love for one another" (John 13:34–35).

Notice that Jesus doesn't say that non-Christians will know we are his disciples by our love *for them*, though that's also true. He says they'll know by our love *for one another*. Interesting, isn't it? How could that be?

Well, look again at the kind of love it is: "just as I have loved you . . ." How did Jesus love us? He loved us with a sin-bearing, self-sacrificing, grace-giving love. "God shows his love for us in that while we were still sinners, Christ died for us" (Rom. 5:8).

What is a church? It's a group of people who know they've been loved by Christ and have begun to love one another like that. This is how Pastor Mark and Dan and Helen and Hardin and Paul and Alice all loved twenty-three-year-old, feet-on-two-horses me.

In fact, this is how our fellow church members love Collin and me today, too—with a forgiving, forbearing, and patient love. And this is how we try to love them in return.

It's a love that the unbelievers out in the world should not only hear about in our words, but also see in our lives together, leading them to say, "We want some, too! Can we join?"

"Ah, friend," we say, "let us first tell you where such love comes from."

Recommended Reading

Dever, Mark. *The Church: The Gospel Made Visible.* Wheaton, IL: Crossway, 2012.

Hill, Megan. *A Place to Belong: Learning to Love the Local Church.* Wheaton, IL: Crossway, 2020.

A church is a group of Christians

↓

who assemble as an earthly embassy
of Christ's heavenly kingdom

↓

to proclaim the good news and
commands of Christ the King;

↓

to affirm one another as his
citizens through the ordinances;

↓

and to display God's
own holiness and love

↓

through a unified and
diverse people

↓

in all the world,

↓

following the teaching
and example of elders.

2

Who Can Belong to a Church?

Collin Hansen

WHEN I WAS GROWING UP, my family often attended church. But not every week. It wasn't a particularly important part of our lives. I imagined that every time we showed up, everyone else was judging us, wondering why we hadn't been there the prior week(s). Maybe they were. Probably they weren't. Most others didn't attend every week either. As I sat in the back with my family, I had a lot of questions about evolution and dinosaurs. I concluded that when my generation took over, we'd leave church behind as a kind of foolish delusion for older generations.

You can imagine my surprise, then, when I started to see other teenagers excited about Jesus and the church. I didn't think it was possible. I assumed you had to be strange, a kind of outcast, to actually enjoy church. But these teenagers seemed happy—and I was not. Unlike me, they seemed to have purpose and hope. I was willing, at least, to attend a church retreat with them.

Still, I struggled to comprehend—What could fill teenagers with such joy?

One day on the retreat, the reason become clear. Apart from faith in Jesus, we stand condemned in our sin, alienated from God. But through Jesus's sacrificial death on the cross, we can receive forgiveness for our sins when we repent or turn away from them. Because Jesus has been raised from the dead, we can enjoy peace and fellowship forever with the God who is three in one: Father, Son, and Holy Spirit.

I can't tell you if I'd ever heard that message before in church. If I had, it hadn't struck me the way it did during this retreat. And I would never be the same again. I had been converted. The change was immediately apparent to my family members and friends—I had joy, freedom, hope. After my experience, many of them believed also.

Later I was baptized and joined a church. Then it made sense why I had such a negative view of church growing up—it was because I had not yet been converted. My family expected dutiful attendance but not wholehearted participation. I had to rediscover church and answer for myself the questions about who can belong and how they become eligible to join.

Who, then, can join a church? Baptized Christians. People who have been born again and then identify as believers through baptism. Admittedly, our paedobaptist friends would say the children of believers can also join a church upon infant baptism (as non-communing or noncommunion-receiving members). Yet everyone agrees that among adults, a person must be born again and baptized to join a church. We'll discuss baptism in chapter 5. Let's think about conversion here and why it's essential to rediscovering church.

Crashing the Holidays

Chances are that those of us who have attended the same church for an extended time don't know how strange it can feel for a visitor. If you don't know anything about church, just walking inside the building demands courage. Where do you go? What do you say? Are you even allowed to enter? Does anyone want or expect you? What are you supposed to wear? As if that's not enough, COVID-19 added questions about whether church is online or in-person, outside or inside, with or without masks—not to mention vaccine expectations.

For someone new to church, the terminology sounds funny. When have you ever heard the term *benediction* outside the church? Where else do you sit in a pew? The music is unfamiliar. You only sing along to an organ today in church or at Wrigley Field. When we sing the same songs as thirty years ago in the church, we call it "contemporary Christian music." On the radio, that's called "oldies." Sometimes even the smell is distinct. Someone could bottle the smell of musty carpet, cheap coffee, hair spray, and snuffed candles, and sell it as nostalgia.

If you can get good answers to your many questions about church, congratulations! Now, you'll find the answers change depending on the church. What's the difference between Baptist, Roman Catholic, Methodist, Presbyterian, and Anglican? And a Baptist church in the United States may not look, sound, or feel like a Baptist church in Uganda.

I once preached at a Pentecostal church in Italy. I prepared a sermon only half as long as my usual thirty minutes since I knew it would need to be translated. When I finished, no one stirred. It dawned on me that I had never asked how long their sermons typically ran. Only later did I realize that they had expected me to teach for an hour. They must've felt cheated. Such customs differ from church to church, from tradition to tradition, and from country to country.

Visiting a church can feel like crashing another family's holiday. Imagine that you decide to knock on someone's door around dinnertime on Christmas Day. All the people there know and love each other (at least they appear to on Christmas). But you're a stranger. Imagine they actually invite you to join in the festivities. Thanks to popular culture, you probably have a general idea of what to expect. There will be food and gifts. But what foods they eat will depend on family traditions taken for granted over generations. How and to whom they give out gifts likewise will follow a pattern fiercely defended by the keepers of family lore. If you make the wrong move, you'll ruin this intimate experience for everyone else.

That's how visiting a church can feel, even if that church would love for you to visit and join. Earlier we likened the church to a spiritual family. What does that mean? To become a part of a family, you need to be either born or adopted. And the Bible actually uses both concepts to describe what's called conversion, which is how you become part of this spiritual family of the church. Just as you don't choose to be born or adopted, so also you don't choose conversion. Let's explore, then, what the Bible teaches about spiritual birth and adoption as necessary for joining the church.

You Must Be Born Again

If you're confused about the concept of spiritual birth, you're not the first. In fact, spiritual birth perplexed one of the first followers of Jesus and led to one of the most well-known exchanges of the

New Testament. The follower's name was Nicodemus, and you can read about him in John 3. He belonged to the Pharisees, a group of especially observant Jews who often clashed with Jesus over interpreting the law. Nicodemus, then, didn't feel comfortable approaching Jesus in the daylight, for fear of being seen with the enemy. But Nicodemus couldn't deny what he'd seen from Jesus. It was obvious that Jesus wouldn't have been able to perform miracles such as turning water into wine at the wedding at Cana unless he had come from God. However, Nicodemus hadn't even formed a question when Jesus dropped this bombshell on him: "Truly, truly, I say to you, unless one is born again he cannot see the kingdom of God" (John 3:3).

Say what? Nicodemus asked the obvious follow-up question: How is that possible? Once you leave your mother, you can't climb back in. Jesus didn't exactly clarify much in his response: "Truly, truly, I say to you, unless one is born of water and the Spirit, he cannot enter the kingdom of God" (John 3:5).

That's the key to our questions in this chapter: Who can visit a church building for a worship service? The answer is, anyone! But who can belong to the spiritual family called the church? Only those who have entered the kingdom of God. Only those who have been born of water and the Spirit, according to Jesus—that is, only those who have been born again and been baptized. And how does that happen? Jesus explained to the baffled Nicodemus: "For God so loved the world, that he gave his only Son, that whoever believes in him should not perish but have eternal life" (John 3:16).

Nicodemus had expected that you could enter the kingdom of God only if you observed God's law and its extensive stipulations on work and rest, clean and unclean food, and various animal sacrifices. Jesus summed up the law in a revolutionary and simple way: believe in me, and I will give my life for you.

Jesus would go on to explain that his eventual death on the cross, which appeared to be his defeat, was actually God's plan to satisfy justice and forgive sin. And he proved it in his resurrection from the dead. All who put their faith in Jesus will follow him after death into heaven. When this world ends, their bodies will be resurrected, and they will enjoy eternity as Jesus reigns in God's kingdom. All who believe in Jesus will be saved from God's judgment for sin. But those who deny him will suffer eternal punishment for disobedience (John 3:36).

Later, the apostle Paul would put it this way: "If you confess with your mouth that Jesus is Lord and believe in your heart that God raised him from the dead, you will be saved" (Rom. 10:9).

The first time we were born, we inherited sin from our parents, going all the way back to the original rebellion of Adam and Eve (Gen. 3). That's why we must be born again, so that we will not die without hope. We need to be saved from the consequences of sin, which are eternal death and separation from God our Creator. But just as we did not ask to be born the first time, only our Creator can cause us to be born again. "Blessed be the God and Father of our Lord Jesus Christ! According to his great mercy, he has caused us to be born again to a living hope through the resurrection of Jesus Christ from the dead" (1 Pet. 1:3).

The faith to believe in Jesus, then, is a gift from God (Eph. 2:8). And it's a gift God delights to give to those who ask. It comes to all who repent or turn away from their sins and put all their faith in nothing and no one but Jesus Christ. When the apostles saw this gift of repentance granted to Gentiles and not only to Jews, they glorified God (Acts 11:18). Following God means forsaking all others. When we're born again, we belong entirely to him. To rediscover church is to realize or remember why we gather in the first place. We gather to worship God—Father, Son, and Holy Spirit—who has saved us from sin and death. That's what we sing. That's what we teach. That's what we observe in baptism and the Lord's Supper.

Without conversion, without being born again, there is no church to rediscover. If Jesus has not died for our sins and been raised on the third day, there is no more hope to be found inside the church than outside.

Adopted as Sons and Daughters

Once, years ago, I was talking with some loved ones about church. They knew I had undergone a powerful conversion experience at age fifteen. When I became born again, everything changed. I got to know God in the Bible and in prayer. I enjoyed singing to and about him. I wanted all my friends to know how they could be born again. Still, some of these loved ones didn't understand, even though they tried. They wanted to relate to me. So they reported to me when they attended church. I knew church didn't mean anything to them, that they just wanted to please me. So I told them to stop going to church. Finally, an idea they liked! They found other ways to spend their Sunday mornings. I just wanted them to understand there is no intrinsic value to attending church if you don't bother to believe what you're singing, hearing, or saying.

I'm not sure I would always recommend "stop going to church" as an evangelistic strategy. But in this case it was necessary, because my loved ones attended a church that did not teach clearly about conversion. Eventually they met a different pastor, who invited them to believe in Jesus and be born again. They began attending his church, where they were baptized. And they've belonged to that spiritual family now for nearly twenty years.

Conversion can happen inside or outside the church. It can be a solitary experience or one you share with friends and peers. But it should always result in you linking together with a church. When the Bible describes our conversion as adoption, we see this corporate dimension. Sometimes the English language obscures how often the Bible speaks of spiritual growth in the plural: where it says *you*, it often means "y'all." A clear example comes in Galatians 4:4–5: "But when the fullness of time had come, God sent forth his Son, born of woman, born under the law, to redeem those who were under the law, so that we might receive adoption as sons." This English translation retains the gender-specific "sons" to reflect their privileged hereditary position in the ancient world. But this promise applies to all men and women who believe in Jesus. When God adopts you, when he gives you the gift of faith in his Son, he welcomes you into a spiritual family of brothers and sisters—that is, the church.

Think about it this way. In adoption, a child gets new parents. But he also gets new siblings. When he becomes a son, he also becomes a brother—two new but distinct relationships. When you become a son, you snag a spot in the family photo next to your siblings. And that's what happens in conversion. Your Father puts you in the family photo with your new kin.

Let's get a closer look at that family photo. God is the Father who "predestined us for adoption" (Eph. 1:5). Before the beginning of time, he gathered this family together across all ages and places. God is the Son, our older brother sent by the Father to rescue us from slavery to sin and death so that we could join the family (Rom. 8:15; Gal. 4:4). God is the Spirit who "bears witness with our spirit that we are children of God" (Rom. 8:16). So in adoption, the family photo is an action shot. Three persons—Father, Son, and Holy Spirit—work together in perfect harmony on our behalf.

And where are we in the photo? As sons and daughters, we are heirs with Christ (Rom. 8:17; Gal. 4:7). That means we share in his inheritance (Eph. 1:11, 14).

What does that include? The apostle Paul tells us in Colossians 1:16 that "all things were created through him and for him." Your great aunt might've been generous, but you can't beat that inheritance.

Families don't always get along. But their bonds to one another as family members help them persevere through conflict. The shared blood prevails. The same is true for the church. Because we've been reconciled to God through repentance and faith, we've also been reconciled to each other. The blood of Christ prevailed in the early church over the divisions between Gentiles and Jews. That divide makes problems in churches today look mild by comparison. But look at the miracle worked by conversion when Jew and Gentile believe the gospel together:

> So then you are no longer strangers and aliens, but you are
> fellow citizens with the saints and members of the household
> of God, built on the foundation of the apostles and prophets,
> Christ Jesus himself being the cornerstone, in whom the whole

structure, being joined together, grows into a holy temple in the Lord. In him you also are being built together into a dwelling place for God by the Spirit. (Eph. 2:19–22)

When a church delights together in the joy of conversion, believers gain perspective on what still divides them. The holy temple of God is not so easily torn down.

Set Apart

One of the greatest responsibilities I enjoy as an elder in my church is interviewing new members. Over the last five years or so, my fellow elders and I have welcomed more than a thousand new members. That means I've heard a lot of conversion stories. I don't meet to interrogate those who are interested in membership, but simply to ensure that they have experienced the conversion we've been discussing in this chapter and can explain it to someone else who wants to be a Christian.

Every person's story is unique in terms of the role of family, church, and youth ministry. Some have engaged in especially wicked sin. Most have not. Rarely do I meet someone who hasn't drifted away from the church for a time. Usually people's faith does not look exactly the same as in the households where they grew up. I enjoy hearing these eclectic stories about God's work of adoption, of how people became born again. It never gets old.

Occasionally I meet someone who wants to be part of our church but clearly has not been born again. Sometimes I'll ask the person to explain the good news or gospel of Jesus, and I might as well have asked my six-year-old son to explain Einstein's theory of relativity. I get nothing but a blank stare. More often I hear a story about church, morality, and trials, but nothing specifically about sin and the saving grace of Jesus. No shift from death to life, from judgment to resurrection.

Where I live, it's fairly common for churches to include many members who have not been converted. Few seem to even understand why that is a problem. But the Bible presents conversion as a transformation that sets apart God's people from the world. It's an eternity-altering experience. This is what the Old Testament writers sometimes referred to as the "new covenant." Speaking for God, the prophet Jeremiah promised Israel, "I will put my law within them, and I will write it on their hearts. And I will be their God, and they shall be my people" (Jer. 31:33). Writing a little bit later and also speaking for God, the prophet Ezekiel anticipated what Jesus would tell Nicodemus: "And I will give you a heart, and a new spirit I will put within you. And I will remove the heart of stone from your flesh and give you a heart of flesh. And I will put my Spirit within you, and cause you to walk in my statutes and be careful to obey my rules" (Ezek. 36:26–27).

Passages like these don't envision the church as a place where people *kinda* try to be good and *kinda* try to help each other out, at least if it's convenient. No, the new covenant penetrates all the way down to our hearts. It makes a radical change. It causes us to turn from our former life and turn toward Christ. It provides the power of the Spirit to obey the law written on new hearts.

Inside the church, we can't know everyone's true spiritual state, what they believe in their heart of hearts. But that doesn't change the Bible's architectural design for our churches—what it *intends* and what our practices should be. If you've been born again, if you have repented of your sins and believe in Jesus, you can belong to the church. You don't need to settle for duty without understanding or purpose, as you daydream along with my younger self about a future without church. When you're converted, you can't help but worship. You look forward to gathering and worshiping with other believers in Jesus.

Speaking of gatherings . . .

Recommended Reading

Keller, Timothy. *Prodigal God: Recovering the Heart of the Christian Faith*. New York: Viking, 2008.

Lawrence, Michael. *Conversion: How God Creates a People*. Wheaton, IL: Crossway, 2017.

A church is a group of Christians

$\downarrow$

**who assemble as an earthly embassy
of Christ's heavenly kingdom**

$\downarrow$

to proclaim the good news and
commands of Christ the King;

$\downarrow$

to affirm one another as his
citizens through the ordinances;

$\downarrow$

and to display God's
own holiness and love

$\downarrow$

through a unified and
diverse people

$\downarrow$

in all the world,

$\downarrow$

following the teaching
and example of elders.

3

Do We Really Need to Gather?

Jonathan Leeman

NEWS OF POLITICAL PROTESTS dominated American headlines in 2020 and early 2021. Folks on the political left said they were protesting police brutality against minorities, while folks on the right said they were protesting a stolen presidential election.

When thousands of citizens gather and march for political purposes, the public pays attention. Reporters show up. Video cameras turn on. Politicians give interviews. And folks at home stare at their phones, clicking link after link after link. Then, after a few weeks have passed, a legislature might pass new laws. A government agency might enact new policies. And a nation's conscience might be changed, if only a little.

Groups of people are powerful, not just for what happens when they gather, but for what that group *becomes* by gathering. The people in the group can become a movement. A force. The beginning of a change in the world, for better or worse. The whole is more than the sum of its parts.

Not surprisingly, academics write books on the psychology of crowds. People show up with their desires or grievances. A charismatic speaker affirms those desires or grievances. The people look around and see heads nodding. They hear shouts of agreement. Individuals discover they're not alone. Their desires grow. They might even be rallied to action, to build up or to tear down.

What makes gatherings so powerful? The fact that you are physically *there*. You see. You hear. You feel. Unlike watching something on a screen, in which you're bodily removed from the thing you're watching, a gathering literally surrounds you. It defines your entire reality. God made us soul and body, and somehow, mysteriously, he intertwines them so that what affects the body affects the soul. In a gathering, we experience what other people love, hate, fear, and believe, and our sense of *what's normal* and *what's right* can shift comparatively quickly. The loves, hates, fears, or beliefs of the crowd become ours. This isn't surprising. God also made us "imaging" creatures (see Gen. 1:26–28). He created us to image his own righteousness, but we've chosen to image other things. This is how cultures form. We image, mimic, or copy the people around us in good ways and bad. Gatherings simply speed up the process.

But gatherings aren't powerful only for people inside of them. They affect outsiders, too. Maybe you've walked through a park, seen a crowd, and craned your neck in that direction. *What's going on?* you wondered. So you walked up to the back of the crowd and peeked in. Why? Because you wondered if something was happening that you didn't want to miss—something important or exciting.

Or you pick up your smartphone and see a news notification: "200,000 gather in Washington, DC, for rally." You think, *Wow, this sounds like a big deal.* And you click the link.

Gatherings change lives, change cultures, change the world. They're powerful.

Churches Gather and Are Gatherings

Like a political protest, the church gathering shapes a people. It shapes each one of us as individuals and shapes us collectively into a culture, a force, or a movement. It fashions us as the city of God. And like a protest, the gathering offers a visible testimony for the whole world to see. It tells the world we are citizens of heaven. *What's going on over there?* they wonder.

A pastor friend of ours recently observed that, when the COVID-19 quarantines ended, his church discovered afresh how profoundly "spiritual" the gathering is. That was the word he used: "spiritual." He's right, our gatherings are spiritual. Yet ironically, they're spiritual, at least in part, because they're physical.

God has always meant for his people to be physically gathered with him. That's why he created Adam and Eve with physical bodies and walked with them in the garden of Eden. He cast them out from his presence only when they sinned.

God then gathered the people of Israel in the promised land and told them to assemble regularly at the temple where he dwelled (e.g., Deut. 16:16; 31:10–12, 30). Again they sinned, and again he cast them out of the land.

Perhaps the clearest proof of God's desire to gather with his people is the incarnation. The Son of God took on a body. The one who was *with* God and who was God (John 1:1–2) put on flesh so that he could be *with* us (John 1:14). And he promised to build his church—a word that, translated literally, means "assembly" (Matt. 16:18).

Maybe you've never wondered why Jesus chose the word "church." The Jews of Jesus's day gathered in synagogues, but Jesus didn't use the word "synagogue." He used the word "church." Why? We can answer this by looking backward and forward in the storyline of the Bible. Looking backward, we learn that it was prophesied that Jesus would assemble a people who had been scattered by exile (see Joel 2:16). Looking forward, we understand that Jesus wanted these assemblies—these churches—to anticipate the final assembly where God will dwell with his people once more: "Behold, the dwelling place of God is with man. He will dwell with them" (Rev. 21:3; also 7:9ff.).

Our assembled local churches represent God's presence with man—where heaven comes to earth. "Where two or three are gathered in my name, there am I among them" (Matt. 18:20; also, v. 17). This doesn't happen on the internet or in our heads. It happens "when you come together as a church," to borrow a phrase from Paul, a phrase that suggests there's a sense in which a church is not a church until it comes together (1 Cor. 11:18).

Sometimes people like to say that "a church is a people, not a place." It's slightly more accurate to say that a church is a people assembled in a place. Regularly assembling or gathering makes a church a church. This doesn't mean a church stops being a church when the people aren't gathered, any more than a soccer "team" stops being a team when the members are not playing. The point is, regularly gathering together is necessary for a church to be a church, just like a team has to gather to play in order to be a team.

Jesus organized Christianity this way. He means to center our Christianity around regularly gathering together, seeing one another, learning from one another, encouraging and correcting one another, and loving one another. Spiritual things happen when Christians stand elbow to elbow, breathe the same air, join our voices in song, hear the same sermon, and partake of the one bread (see 1 Cor. 10:17). You look around and think, *I'm not alone in this faith. What might we do together?*

That's a lot of theology. But it comes with a lesson. It explains why the author of Hebrews writes,

> And let us consider how to stir up one another to love and good works, not neglecting to meet together, as is the habit of some, but encouraging one another, and all the more as you see the Day drawing near.
>
> For if we go on sinning deliberately after receiving the knowledge of the truth, there no longer remains a sacrifice for sins, but a fearful expectation of judgment, and a fury of fire that will consume the adversaries. (Heb. 10:24–27)

In the gathering, we stir one another up to love and good works. We encourage one another. And notice the author's warning: if we go on sinning by not doing these things—including not gathering—we should expect God's judgment. Goodness! He takes this seriously.

The point is not that attending church *makes* you a Christian. The point is that attending church is what Christians do. It demonstrates that the Spirit of Christ is in us, and therefore we desire to be with Christ's people.

Centered on God's Word

A couple chapters ago, I recounted that I switched from not attending church to attending three times a week when I moved to Washington, DC. Before those days, I had avoided God's people and was even a little embarrassed to be seen around them. Yet suddenly and strangely, I *wanted* to be with them. Every week, I looked forward to being with the church.

What animated this change? Most prominently, I wanted to hear from God. After all, *that's* what makes church gatherings distinct from political protests or any other assembly—we gather around the very words of God: "When you received the word of God, which you heard from us, you accepted it not as the word of men but as what it really is, the word of God, which is at work in you believers" (1 Thess. 2:13). In the church gathering, God speaks, and citizens of planet earth can hear from God and see a people growing up around his Word. When unbelievers step into the gathering, Paul promises, they will be convicted of sin, the secrets of their hearts will be laid bare, and they will fall down and worship God, exclaiming, "God is really among you!" (see 1 Cor. 14:24–25).

Challenge of COVID-19—Not Gathering

The COVID-19 pandemic was challenging for churches around the world precisely because, in so many places, the saints had difficulty gathering and learning to cherish the words of God together. After a couple of months of not gathering during the early days of COVID-19, I felt as if I was losing track of my church. Friends would ask, "How is your church doing?" I had a hard time answering. I was making regular phone calls and sending text messages to individual members, but I couldn't get my mind around the whole body. The church felt like rainwater on a parking lot after a storm—spread thin, with puddles here and there.

The elders worried most about the spiritually weak members who were struggling in their faith or facing particular temptations. We worried about those who already seemed to be drifting spiritually, those with one foot out the door.

Yet not gathering affected everyone—the spiritually mature and immature alike. Each one of us needs to see and to hear our fellow saints on a regular basis. Otherwise, it's only colleagues at work, friends at school, or TV characters whose patterns we observe.

Once the pandemic began, many churches livestreamed their services, and many voices extolled the enduring value of "virtual church." Pastors who had previously decried the idea now opened up "virtual campuses" and staffed them with full-time pastors, promising that the campuses would continue indefinitely. This was an exciting development in the history of fulfilling the Great Commission, some said.

And yet, we wonder: What goes missing when your "church" experience is nothing more than a weekly livestream? For starters, you think less about your fellow members. They don't come to mind. You don't bump into them and have the quick conversations that lead to longer conversations over dinner. Beyond that, you remove yourself from the path of encouragement, accountability, and love.

Praise God that we can "download" biblical truths virtually. But let's praise God that the Christian life is more than just an information transfer. When church is only online, we can't feel, experience, and witness those truths becoming enfleshed in the family of God, which both fortifies our faith and creates cords of love between brothers and sisters. Virtual church is an oxymoron.

Think about it. Maybe you struggle with hidden hatred toward a brother all week. But then his presence at the Lord's Table draws you to conviction and confession. You struggle with suspicion toward a sister. But then you see her singing the same songs of praise, and your heart warms. You struggle with anxiety over what's happening politically in your nation. But then the preacher declares Christ's coming in victory and vindication, you hear shouts of "Amen!" all around you, and you recall that you belong to a heavenly citizenry allied in hope. You're tempted to keep your struggle in the dark. But then the older couple's tender but pressing question over lunch—"How are you *really?*"—draws you into the light.

None of this can be experienced virtually. God made us physical and relational creatures. The Christian life and the church life cannot finally be downloaded. It must be watched, heard, stepped into, and followed. Paul therefore exhorted Timothy to watch his life and doctrine, since both would be crucial to saving himself and his hearers (1 Tim. 4:16).

It's no surprise that virtual, or internet, church is growing in popularity. It's convenient and—honestly—it allows you to avoid messy relationships. We get it; that's a strong temptation. When I was still single, I moved to another city. I didn't have a church or know anyone. A few days after arriving, the thought flashed through my mind, *I can go out and do whatever I want. Nobody is here to see, hear, or ask. That's kind of nice.* Thankfully, the Spirit immediately rebuked me: "You know where that thought comes from. No, that's not an impulse to follow." What grace! The Spirit gratefully checked my heart that day. Yet don't miss the lesson: ordinarily he means to use brothers and sisters in the church to help us fight folly and temptation.

Yes, gathering with the church can be inconvenient, but so is love. Relationships are messy, but so is love. Vulnerable conversations are scary, but so is love.

The push toward the virtual church, we fear, is a push to individualize Christianity. We can debate the wisdom of using such a tool for a limited time in an emergency situation, such as a pandemic. Coastal cities in the United States couldn't meet Sunday evenings during World War II due to government-imposed blackouts. Fair enough. Yet to offer or encourage the virtual church as a permanent option, even with good intentions, hurts Christian discipleship. It trains Christians to think of their faith in autonomous terms. It teaches them that they can follow Jesus as a member of the "family of God," in some abstract sense, without teaching them what it means to be a part of a family and to make sacrifices for a family.

In that regard, pastors should encourage people away from virtual "attendance" as much as they are able. I recently said to my fellow elders, "Brothers, we need to find a gentle way to remind our members that the livestream option is not good for them. It's not good for their discipleship, and it's not good for their faith. We want this to be clear to them, lest they become complacent and not work hard at gathering with us, if they can." The Bible's command to gather is not meant to be burdensome (see Heb. 10:25; 1 John 5:3), but for the good of our faith, our love, and our joy.

Embassy of Heaven

We began this chapter by comparing the church gathering to a protest. But there's a better metaphor that will set us up well for the next chapters. Gathered churches are *embassies of heaven*.

An embassy is an officially sanctioned outpost of one nation inside the borders of another nation. It represents and speaks for that foreign nation. It represents its government. For instance, if you ever visit Washington, DC, you can walk down Embassy Row, where embassy after embassy from around the world is lined up. You'll see the Japanese flag and embassy, then the United Kingdom's, then Italy's, then Finland's. Each embassy represents a nation of the world and its government. Were you to enter one of these embassies, you would hear the language of the nation it represents. Among its staff, you would experience its culture. If you attended an embassy dinner, you'd taste its delicacies. And if you sneaked into the back offices—we assume—you'd learn about its diplomatic business.

What's a gathered church? It's an embassy of heaven. Step inside your church or ours, and what should you find? A whole different nation—sojourners, exiles, citizens of Christ's kingdom. Inside such churches, you'll hear the King of heaven's words declared. You'll hear heaven's language of faith, hope, and love. You'll get a taste of the end-time heavenly banquet through the Lord's Supper. And you'll be charged with its diplomatic business as you're called to bring the gospel to your nation and every other nation.

Not only that, you should experience the beginning of heaven's culture. The heavenly citizens in this embassy are poor in spirit and meek. As they follow Christ, they hunger and thirst for righteousness. They're pure in heart. They're peacemakers who turn the other cheek, walk the extra mile, and give their shirt and jacket if you ask. They won't even look at a woman lustfully, much less commit adultery; they won't even hate, much less commit murder.

Jesus didn't ask the United Nations, the U.S. Supreme Court, or the Oxford University philosophy department to represent him and declare his judgments. He asked the humble, the lowly, the "things that are not" (1 Cor. 1:28). He asked your church and ours.

Sadly, our churches won't always declare and embody heaven well. We'll disappoint you and say insensitive things. We'll even sin against you. Our assemblies are merely signs and foreshadowings of that future heavenly assembly, just as the little wafers we receive in the Lord's Supper are signs of a heavenly banquet. They aren't the things themselves. Yet we aspire to point you to the heart of heaven, who is Christ himself. He never sins or disappoints. The good news is that sinners like you can join us in that enterprise, if you'll only confess your sins and follow after him.

Recommended Reading

Kim, Jay Y. *Analog Church: Why We Need Real People, Places, and Things in the Digital Age.* Downers Grove, IL: InterVarsity Press, 2020.

Leeman, Jonathan. *One Assembly: Rethinking the Multisite and Multi-service Church Models.* Wheaton, IL: Crossway, 2020.

A church is a group of Christians

↓

who assemble as an earthly embassy
of Christ's heavenly kingdom

↓

**to proclaim the good news and
commands of Christ the King;**

↓

to affirm one another as his
citizens through the ordinances;

↓

and to display God's
own holiness and love

↓

through a unified and
diverse people

↓

in all the world,

↓

following the teaching
and example of elders.

4

Why Are Preaching and Teaching Central?

Collin Hansen

WHAT GIVES ANY PREACHER the right to stand up at least once a week for, say, half an hour and claim to speak on behalf of God? Not even the president of the United States boasts such authority. No one thinks a math teacher or literature professor deserves this privilege. And how many other one-directional monologues do you regularly encounter these days anyway? What was once popular, the stuff of itinerant entertainment in the ancient world, would scarcely draw a crowd in any city center today, let alone pave the way toward a lucrative career in public speaking.

Preachers draw their authority not from superior knowledge, political power, or rhetorical flourish. They draw it from God's Word alone. "Preach the word," Paul told his young disciple Timothy, the pastor in Ephesus; "be ready in season and out of season; reprove, rebuke, and exhort, with complete patience and teaching" (2 Tim. 4:2).

Preachers don't have authority if they're reviewing the latest Netflix series. They don't have authority if you're asking for a restaurant recommendation. They don't have authority if they're sharing thoughts about a conspiracy theory they saw on Facebook. They might make some good, interesting, or worthwhile points. They might have some good advice if you need, say, help finding a job. But they derive special authority to speak on God's behalf only when they preach his Word.

No one is a better preacher than Jesus. And no one can preach a better message than his Sermon on the Mount. Its truth and power still change lives and move us today. But it also struck his original hearers as different from what they normally heard from teachers. Matthew tells us, "And when Jesus finished these sayings, the crowds were astonished at his teaching, for he was teaching them as one who had authority, and not as their scribes" (Matt. 7:28–29). The scribes were the official teachers of Israel. So why didn't the crowds respect their authority? It was because they taught their own thoughts. They added their own laws to God's law. Jesus, being God himself, taught with authority as one who wrote and obeyed the law perfectly.

As we rediscover church, we're looking for divine authority and not merely human wisdom. We have more than enough human wisdom today. You've never had such widespread access. Self-help books dominate bestseller lists. Podcasts promise a better you. You'll never reach the end of the internet. So a church that offers human wisdom meets stiff competition. Why listen to a local pastor instead of subscribing to a YouTube channel? Why get up on Sunday morning instead of watching the news programs featuring powerful politicians?

We get up and gather with the church weekly because that's where we hear from the divine King—his good news and his counsel for our lives. We hear from him every time we open our Bibles, yes, but we hear from him *together* in the weekly gathering. We're shaped *together* as a people there. This is why preaching and teaching are central to our church gatherings. Centering our gatherings around God's Word cultivates the heavenly culture that should characterize us as a distinct people, so that we can, in turn, be salt and light in our separate cities and nations.

With the Spirit's help, you know divine wisdom when you hear it. And it's not like the human wisdom of today's self-appointed scribes, who are so common on social media and in bestselling books. The preacher's authority covers all God has said but does not go beyond what God has said. Preachers may be guilty of saying too much or too little. That means the Word is the basis but also the limit of the sermon.

Mark Dever often compares the preacher's work to the task of a mail carrier. The mail carrier doesn't walk up to your door, open up the mail, jot down a few extra notes, reseal the envelope, and then place the letter in your mailbox. A mail carrier simply delivers the mail.

So it is with a preacher. The Word helps us discern his proper authority. He has the authority to deliver the mail. Nothing else.

Self-help gurus lack authority because they have a vested interest in telling you what you want to hear—otherwise, you won't buy their products and subscribe to their programs. Such scribes go beyond God's Word and claim authority that does not belong to them. They seek to bind your conscience on matters that cannot be determined from Scripture alone. They might try to tell you whom to date, whom to vote for, where to enroll your children in school, or what kind of clothing indicates godliness. In all these things, they may truly pass along wisdom, but we must not equate good advice with divine authority. The sermon is not the place for human reflections but divine power.

Thus Says the Lord

Throughout the Old Testament, the prophets echoed a refrain: "Thus says the Lord." They spoke with authority because God entrusted his message to them. They spoke on his behalf. That means the prophets did not always say what the people wanted to hear. In fact, it was common for kings to punish the prophets when they didn't like what they heard.

For instance, King Zedekiah allowed the prophet Jeremiah to be tossed into a cistern and left to die of starvation (Jer. 38:9). Why did the king do this? Jeremiah had told the Jews in Jerusalem that if they stayed in the city, the Chaldeans would kill them. He was right, of course. But that wasn't what the king and his military commanders wanted to hear. It was bad for morale (vv. 2–4). They blamed the messenger so that they wouldn't have to heed the message. They preferred prophets who told comforting lies. God, on the other hand, was not amused by the lying: "Behold, I will feed them with bitter food / and give them poisoned water to drink, / for from the prophets of Jerusalem / ungodliness has gone out into all the land" (23:15).

Through his prophet Ezekiel, God rebuked the leaders, or "shepherds," of Israel who lied to the people they had been commanded to protect: "Ah, shepherds of Israel who have been feeding yourselves! Should not shepherds feed the sheep? You eat the fat, you clothe yourselves with the wool, you slaughter the fat ones, but you do not feed the sheep" (Ezek. 34:2–3).

The experiences of Israel warn that as we rediscover church, we're prone to seek out leaders who tell us only what we want to hear. And leaders are tempted to give the people what they want, because it's easier to make a living that way. It's even possible for preachers to sound like bold truth tellers when they only speak harshly about people outside their churches. They may sound courageous, but they never actually challenge the people who pay their bills.

In fact, that might be the greatest challenge most preachers face. How can they preach the Bible and nothing but the Bible without stepping on more than a few toes? How can they say hard and truthful things to people who control their livelihoods and could remove them and their families from their houses and communities?

Teach the Word to Yourself

Given this temptation for preachers, it's important for the rest of us to make ourselves willing to hear and heed the Word, even if we don't always like it or agree with it at first. As you rediscover church, you're looking for preachers who will not just make you depend on them for hidden biblical insights, but will show you how to teach yourself the Word.

The best preachers don't make you marvel at their own skill. They show you God's glory as seen in his Word. And when you see God that way, you want as much of him as you can get. You grow in eagerness to read and apply the Word for yourself. Then you enter a virtuous feedback loop. The more preachers help you know and love the Word, the more you develop that taste for yourself, and the better taste you develop for meaty preaching.

That relationship between preachers and church members is the key to any healthy church because there is never just one teacher in the church. All of us have been called to teach the Word in some capacity. For instance, all elders, and not just the preacher, must be "able to teach" as part of their leadership (1 Tim. 3:2). Parents teach the Word to their children (Deut. 6:7). Older women teach younger women (Titus 2:3–5).

Think about the work of the Word in a church through at least four movements: (1) the preacher brings the Word for the whole church; (2) the church members respond by taking God's Word into their mouths and hearts through the singing and corporate prayers; (3) all members of the church teach the Word to themselves; and (4) various members of the church teach the Word to one another and to the next generation. That means every member of the church has been called in some capacity as a student and also a teacher of the Word.

With this view of the Word, churches protect themselves from one of the most common problems today, which the biblical writers anticipated and endured themselves. Paul told Timothy to warn the Ephesians not "to devote themselves to myths and endless genealogies, which promote speculations rather than the stewardship from God that is by faith" (1 Tim. 1:4). In Paul's second letter to Timothy, he likewise warned, "For the time is coming when people will not endure sound teaching, but having itching ears they will accumulate for themselves teachers to suit their own passions, and will turn away from listening to the truth and wander off into myths" (2 Tim. 4:3–4). We see, then, that a church focused on the Word will be less interested in "their own passions," speculation that gives the appearance of knowledge but actually indicates foolishness. Paul might have thought Satan himself created the internet as a tool to divide and distract churches with endless speculation.

Think about the preacher's unique challenge today. He might command as much as forty-five or even sixty minutes of your attention this week. And that's if your attention isn't divided by children, drowsiness, and text messages popping up while you're trying to watch the sermon at home. But social media, videos, and podcasts command seemingly every spare moment around work, driving, and sleeping. No wonder it feels as if our churches can't get on the same page! We're not prioritizing the same pages of Scripture. The churches that will emerge strongest through the aftermath of COVID-19 will be those that differentiated between God's Word preached in power and the countless other words that vied for our dwindling attention.

What Is a Good Sermon?

As you rediscover church, you may encounter a variety of sermon styles and lengths. You won't find in the Bible any clear formulas. All of the Bible is inspired by God, but you still get a sense for the different authors' personalities. Paul doesn't sound like Peter, who doesn't sound like John. You may prefer your sermons with emotional fervor. You may prefer your sermons with copious references to Hebrew and Greek. Either or both approaches in the same sermon can be used by God to move us toward love and obedience.

You may also hear preachers debate whether sermons should be topical or expositional. Some situations may warrant topical sermons on an upcoming election, a global pandemic, or racial injustice, to cite just three topics of recent interest. But too many topical messages risks eroding preachers' authority by tempting them to tweak the Bible's meaning to make their points. It's better, we believe, to make the steady diet of the church expositional sermons, which *expose* the text by making the point of the biblical passage the point of the message. As many a preacher has said, Paul doesn't command preachers just to preach, but to preach the *Word*.

Preaching that moves sequentially week after week through verses and chapters of the Bible also lets God, not the preacher, set the agenda. Remember, the preacher is a mail carrier delivering the mail. "This week we're going to learn whatever God has for us in Romans 1, next week Romans 2, and the week following Romans 3." When we hear the Bible this way, we discover that God's agenda does not neatly align with ours. There might be things in Romans, for instance, that a preacher doesn't feel like preaching. But there the envelope sits, a letter from God, asking to be opened.

After all, whose agenda do we really want—ours or God's? His ways are higher and better (Isa. 55:9). We should take our cues from him and not from the world. Something special happens when you hear the Spirit speak through God's Word when, to all appearances, the preacher is just picking up where he left off the week before.

When you rediscover church, you'll likely also encounter the debate between recorded and live, in-person sermons. Years ago,

I had a conversation with an especially gifted preacher. In another life, he would have been a successful stand-up comedian. In fact, he studied comedians in order to learn how to engage with an audience while preaching. He also understood biblical and theological concepts with depth and could explain them with creativity to skeptical crowds. His church had expanded to several locations across the region and even the country by broadcasting his recorded sermons rather than featuring local, in-person preachers. I'll never forget his rationale. He said it didn't make sense to give the people a B- preacher when they could have an A preacher like himself. If his goal was to amass a large personal following, I couldn't argue with him.

But as I reflected later, I realized that his argument proved too much. In the scenario he suggested, he wasn't competing only against his junior pastors and interns. He was competing against every other preacher, dead or alive. Why not play recordings of an A+ preacher, such as Billy Graham? What if churches across the English-speaking world hired an actor to perform the best of Charles Spurgeon? Maybe we could compile a tournament bracket of the kind used for college basketball playoffs and ask Christians to vote, round by round, on their favorite preacher until we settled on one orator to rule them all. Then no one would be subject to a B- (or worse) preacher ever again. We'd get only the best—if that's what God thinks is best for us.

But it's not. The best preacher for you is the preacher who is faithful to God's Word. Even better if he's willing to meet you over coffee or visit you in the hospital. There's a reason we don't only read Scripture together in each worship service. Preaching brings the authority of God's Word to bear, through the mediating personality and experience of the teacher, on a contemporary context with particular local and personal demands. The man I just mentioned might in fact be a better preacher than yours, but your preacher knows your church better. And that counts for a lot when it comes to applying the Bible to you and your congregation.

To be sure, pastors can't know all the intimate details of every person in their hearing. But there's a reason so many pastors struggled to preach into a camera during the COVID-19 lockdowns. They pray to sense the Spirit's moving in our real-time reactions to their preaching. When they see us eye to eye, the Spirit calls to their minds comfort for our woes. There are many reasons a church should not dim the lights over the congregation during worship services, as if emulating a concert or movie theater. And this is one of them: so that pastors can respond with sensitivity to the prompting of the Spirit in the act of preaching.

Time and Space

In the end, preaching isn't just about transmitting information. If that were the only goal, then preaching would no longer be the most efficient means to do so. We could move to video, podcasts, or even just books and cut out the worship service altogether. Yet hearing the sermon isn't just about you and your personal walk with Jesus. It's also about shaping a heavenly culture and building a heavenly city in your very church. It's about shaping a life together.

Two things happen with live, in-person teaching that can't be replicated on a podcast with a pastor you'll never know personally. First, the congregation and the preacher together experience preaching as a communal event in time and space. Yes, there's value in applying a sermon alone in our devotional reflections. But there's even more value in applying it to us together as a people. Together we bring the sermon to life in how we treat one another throughout the week. Also, remember, the preacher isn't finally "over" us. He's one of us, and he participates with us in being shaped together by God's Word as a new city. The sermon casts a vision from God's Word for a particular people in a particular place, as they have covenanted together to obey God and love one another.

That said, second, the preacher's example and personality set a tone for the whole congregation. Preachers understandably get scared when they realize how their churches will take on their own weaknesses as well as strengths. When I was learning in seminary about how to preach, my professor offered sobering words. He told me that over the years my congregation would probably not remember the actual words I said. Rather, God would shape a church through both my words and also my example of godliness and integrity over time. The preacher's character and message meld together, and, by the power of the Spirit, hearers are changed by those words, even if they don't always remember them. And that's common for teaching, not just preaching. We don't typically remember our best teachers just for their knowledge. We remember their wisdom alongside their gifting to communicate and their love for us personally.

So as you rediscover church, look for preachers who love you enough that they know how to both cut and stitch you up as necessary, like a good surgeon. Look for ones who know they derive their authority from the King of kings, whose good news and counsel they proclaim. They don't just want a slice of your paycheck. They aim to set an example for you and not merely impress you with their learning and charisma.

Recommended Reading

Leeman, Jonathan. *Word-Centered Church: How Scripture Brings Life and Growth to God's People*. Chicago: Moody, 2017.

Wilkin, Jen. *Women of the Word: How to Study the Bible with Both Our Hearts and Our Minds*. Wheaton, IL: Crossway, 2014.

A church is a group of Christians

↓

who assemble as an earthly embassy
of Christ's heavenly kingdom

↓

to proclaim the good news and
commands of Christ the King;

↓

**to affirm one another as his
citizens through the ordinances;**

↓

and to display God's
own holiness and love

↓

through a unified and
diverse people

↓

in all the world,

↓

following the teaching
and example of elders.

5

Is Joining Actually Necessary?

Jonathan Leeman

IN COLLEGE, I SPENT HALF a year in Brussels, Belgium. During that time, my United States passport expired. So I traveled to the U.S. embassy in the Quartier Royal neighborhood of Brussels. Stepping inside the embassy placed me on American soil.

The embassy bears the authority of the U.S. government. It can say to the government and people of Belgium, "This is what the United States requests and what it intends." It can say of people like me, "He is one of ours."

Standing at the counter, I handed the clerk my expired passport. He asked me a few questions. He typed a few things into his computer. In no time, I received a new passport affirming that I am a U.S. citizen. The embassy didn't *make* me a citizen. I was a citizen by birth. But it did officially recognize and affirm my citizenship. It speaks for the United States in a way that I cannot, even though I am a U.S. citizen.

Do Churches Really Have Authority?

Likewise, churches don't *make* people Christians. We become Christians by the new birth, as we talked about in chapter 2. But churches are embassies of heaven, which Christ has tasked with affirming our heavenly citizenship. Baptists, Presbyterians, and Anglicans might disagree on who exactly makes the pronouncement, whether it is the whole congregation or the elders or bishop acting on behalf of the congregation. But all agree that Jesus has given this authority to churches. Instead of handing out passports, churches baptize and share the Lord's Supper.

Christians today don't often think of churches as possessing a God-given authority. Parents? Yes. Governments? Yes. But churches?

In fact, this is what we learn from Jesus giving the keys of the kingdom to churches in Matthew 16 and 18. First, in Matthew 16:13–20, Jesus teaches that the keys are used to affirm *right confessions of the gospel.* Peter confesses whom Jesus is. Jesus affirms Peter's answer, promises to build his church, and then, for that purpose, gives Peter and the apostles "the keys of the kingdom of heaven" (v. 19). What do these keys do? They bind and loose on earth what's bound and loosed in heaven. We don't talk like that anymore, so you might miss the meaning. But think of the keys as being like an embassy's authority to formally declare its home government's laws or decrees.

Second, in Matthew 18:15–20, Jesus teaches that the keys are used to affirm *true confessors of the gospel.* He hands the keys of the kingdom to a local church as the grounds for removing from membership anyone whose life and profession don't match. Think of this being like an embassy's authority to formally declare who its citizens are.

To summarize, churches possess the keys of the kingdom, which is the authority to affirm on behalf of heaven the *what* and the *who* of the gospel—What is a right confession? Who is a true confessor?

The authority of the keys = the right to declare on Jesus's behalf the *what* and the *who* of the gospel: What is a right confession? Who is a true confessor?

Another analogy that might be helpful for understanding a church's authority of the keys is the work of a courtroom judge. A judge doesn't make the law. Neither does he or she make a person innocent or guilty. But the judge possesses authority on behalf of the government to interpret the law and then render an official judgment: "Guilty" or "Not guilty." So it is with a church's declarations. They're official, representing the kingdom of heaven on earth.

Sometimes churches make wrong judgments, as with ambassadors and embassies, or judges and courts. Still, this is the job that Jesus gives to churches.

What Are the Ordinances? Our Heavenly Passports
How do churches render these official judgments?

First, they do it through preaching, which we talked about in the previous chapter. When the preacher preaches, he "binds" or "looses" the consciences of the congregation to his understanding of God's Word.

Second, churches bind or loose through the *ordinances* (as in, *ordained* by Jesus).

Baptism comes first. It's the front door into church membership. Those who gather in Christ's name (Matt. 18:20) baptize people into his name (28:19). Through baptism, we declare, "I'm with Jesus," while the church affirms, "This person is with Jesus." Both parties have something to say.

The Lord's Supper follows. It's the regular family meal for members (see Matt. 26:26–29). Church membership, in one sense, simply means membership at the Lord's Table, since the Supper is how we recognize one another as believers on an ongoing basis. Listen to Paul: "Because there is one bread, we who are many are one body, for we all partake of the one bread" (1 Cor. 10:17). Partaking of the one bread shows that we are one body. It affirms us as believers. Again, different Christian denominations disagree on what exactly the communion bread represents. But all agree that the Lord's Supper is a church meal, by which the whole congregation affirms one another's membership in Christ's body.

Too often, Christians treat the ordinances individualistically. We practice baptism and the Supper at home, at camp, or on overseas tours. Remaining at home through COVID-19 especially tempted people to think this way.

It's true that the New Testament doesn't absolutely restrict baptism to church settings, as seen in Philip baptizing the Ethiopian eunuch (Acts 8:26–40). A missionary religion pushing into new territories needs to be able to do this. Yet the normal practice is to celebrate these two ordinances within the church gathering under the church's watchful care, as when three thousand were baptized "into" the Jerusalem church (Acts 2:41). Likewise, Paul warns us to participate in the Supper only while "discerning the body," meaning the church (1 Cor. 11:29). Then he tells us to "wait for one another" before taking it (v. 33). This is a church event.

On one occasion when I was taking the Supper with the church, I said to the brothers around me, "As we partake, let's look at one another and then hug at the end." I wanted to capture the corporate nature of what we were doing. My friends groaned at my request, but they agreed. So we huddled up, took the Supper, looked at one another, and then hugged. It felt a little weird, honestly. The guys chuckled. I'm not recommending the practice, per se. But I am trying to illustrate this point: the Lord's Supper is a family meal, not an individual one.

What Is Church Membership?

So what exactly *is* church membership?

Church membership is how we formally recognize and commit to one another as believers. It's the thing we create by affirming one another through the ordinances. To offer a definition, church membership is a church's *affirmation* and *oversight* of a Christian's profession of faith and discipleship, combined with the Christian's *submission* to the church and its oversight. You might think of it like this:

Church membership is

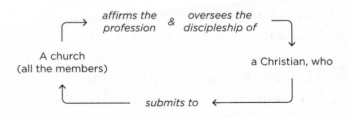

A church
(all the members)

affirms the
profession

&

oversees the
discipleship of

a Christian, who

submits to

The word *submits* is scary, perhaps especially when applied to the church. But it must be said. When you become a church member, you're not just submitting to the leaders or the "institution" in some vague bureaucratic sense. You're submitting to a family and all its members. It's your way of saying, "This is the particular group of Christians I'm inviting into my life and asking to keep me accountable for following Jesus. I'm asking them to take responsibility for my Christian walk. If I'm discouraged, it's now their responsibility to encourage me. If I stray from the narrow path, it's their responsibility to correct me. If I'm in dire financial straits, it's their responsibility to look after me."

Yet this commitment goes both ways. In asking the other members of the church to look out for you, you also are promising to look out for them. You are now a part of the "church" on the left side of the figure above, which is affirming and overseeing others. We'll come back to this point in a moment.

What should also be evident—if you've been paying close attention—is that baptism, the Lord's Supper, and church membership belong together. Exceptions exist, yet ordinarily churches baptize people into membership, and the Lord's Supper is a privilege of church members, whether at one's own church or when visiting another. After all, all three things work together to do the same thing: affirm and mark off the people of God. Together they declare to the nations of the earth, "Here are the citizens of the kingdom of heaven."

Isn't It Enough to Belong to the Universal Church?

Sometimes people like to say, "I don't need to join a church. I already belong to Christ's universal church." (The universal church is what theologians call the entire body of Christ throughout the world and throughout all history.) Is that right? Can we forget about the local church since we all become members of the universal church upon conversion?

The short answer is no. It's true you *don't need* to join a church to be saved. Our membership in the universal church is a gift (Eph. 2:11–22), just as our righteousness in Christ is a gift and faith is a gift. Yet you *do need* to join a church to be obedient to Scripture. Just as our faith should "put on" good works (Col. 3:10, 12; James 2:14–16), so we should "put on" our universal membership locally. Our membership in the universal church cannot remain an abstract idea. If it's real, it will show up on earth—in real time and space with real people with names like Betty, Jamar, Saeed, and Ling. Pandemic lockdowns don't change any of that.

If the Spirit is in you, you want to commit to Christ's body. You almost can't help it. Genuine membership in the universal church creates local church membership, which in turn demonstrates our universal membership, like this:

Relationship between universal and local church membership

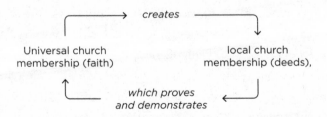

Perhaps, like us, you've had friends who tried to live out their Christianity apart from a church, and little by little their faith shriveled, sometimes disappeared entirely. I had a friend whom I encouraged to join my church after he had been attending for several months. He declined because he didn't want the accountability. Meanwhile, he was dabbling in significant sin. Unsurprisingly, his attendance grew more and more sporadic, until he stopped attending altogether. Finally, he told me one day over coffee, "Jonathan, I'm no longer a Christian, or at least not your kind of Christian."

Church membership offers the safety of the sheep pen, where Christ is shepherd. It offers the nourishment of being attached to a body, like an arm to a torso, where Christ is the head. It offers the love of a family, where Christ is the firstborn of many heirs. It offers the obligations and duties of citizenship in a holy nation, where Christ is the King.

Is Church Membership Really Biblical?

Another question people ask is whether church membership is even in the Bible. Maybe you've asked it yourself.

If we had only the length of an elevator ride with you to answer, we'd point to passages such as Matthew 18:17 and 1 Corinthians 5:2, where Jesus and Paul talk about removing someone from the church's membership, or what Paul says about being "inside" the church (v. 12). Or we'd point to Acts 2 and what Luke says about three thousand people being "added" to the church in Jerusalem (v. 41), or Acts 6 and what he says about calling the church together (v. 2). No, the term "church membership" isn't used in the Bible like we use it today. But the practice is implied nearly every time the word *church* is used in the New Testament, as when Luke says, "Earnest prayer for him was made to God by the church"

(12:5), or Paul writes to "the churches of Galatia" (Gal. 1:2). Though they didn't use all the tools we might use today, such as membership classes, membership packets, and names listed on a computer spreadsheet, they knew who they were—name by name.

Yet there's the bigger story that's important for you to see in order to understand God's larger purposes for churches like yours or ours. Throughout the Bible, God always draws a bright line around his people. The garden of Eden had an inside and an outside. The ark had an inside and outside. The people of Israel in Egypt, quarantined off in Goshen, had an inside and outside. Just think about the plagues themselves. Some targeted just the Egyptians, not God's people. God said,

> But on that day I will set apart the land of Goshen, where my people dwell, so that no swarms of flies shall be there, that you may know that I am the LORD in the midst of the earth. Thus I will put a division between my people and your people. (Ex. 8:22–23)

Flies! God used flies to draw the line between his people and not his people! Then Israel traveled into the wilderness, and he gave them cleanliness laws in order to draw a line between the inside and outside of the camp. Unclean people had to go outside of the camp. Finally, he placed them in the promised land, which had an inside and an outside.

God has always marked off his people so that he might put them on display for his own glory. He wants these embassies to stand out. It's no wonder Paul picks up this Old Testament language when he says,

Do not be unequally yoked with unbelievers. For what partnership has righteousness with lawlessness? Or what fellowship has light with darkness? What accord has Christ with Belial? Or what portion does a believer share with an unbeliever? What agreement has the temple of God with idols? For we are the temple of the living God; as God said,

> "I will make my dwelling among them and walk among
>   them,
>   and I will be their God,
>   and they shall be my people.
> Therefore go out from their midst,
>   and be separate from them, says the Lord,
> and touch no unclean thing;
>   then I will welcome you,
> and I will be a father to you,
>   and you shall be sons and daughters to me,
> says the Lord Almighty." (2 Cor. 6:14–18)

When people ask whether church membership is in the Bible, they're often looking for something programmatic, like membership to a gym or club. And, true enough, that's not in the Bible. Let's remove such ideas from our heads. Instead, let's get into our minds "the temple of the living God," which is the image Paul uses to describe who we are. This temple cannot be "yoked with" or have "partnership," "fellowship," or "accord" with unbelievers. Why? Because God dwells in this temple. He identifies himself with it. Yes, we should still invite nonbelievers into our worship gatherings (1 Cor. 14:24–25). But the point is, a church must be clear about who belongs to it and who doesn't precisely for the sake of the church's witness. He wants us to stand out and be distinct so that we can offer an attractive and compelling witness to the world.

As such, church membership is an assumed reality on nearly every page of the New Testament Epistles, but the language is different. Membership in the church is membership in a family. It comes with family obligations. It's membership in a body. It comes with all the dynamics of being connected to every other part. Every biblical metaphor for the church helps us to understand what membership is, and all of them are necessary, because there is nothing else in the world like the church.

Membership Is a Job

So let's return once more to the idea of a church being an embassy or outpost of the kingdom of heaven. Here's the last thing we want to say in this chapter: membership isn't just a status. It's an office or a job—and you're expected to show up for work (Heb. 10:24–25).

Remember how I walked into the U.S. embassy in Brussels, Belgium, handed in my expired passport, and then was given a new one? Suppose that, upon giving me a new passport, the embassy then put me to work checking passports myself. That's what church membership does: it puts you to work protecting, affirming, and declaring the *what* and *who* of the gospel. It gives you an office.

Where did this office come from? It's interesting to trace the origins of the office because doing so helps you to see how the whole Bible hangs together. Think back to God's command to Adam in Genesis 1 to be fruitful, multiply, and rule over the earth (v. 28). He was to be a *king* (see also Ps. 8). Then think of God's Genesis 2 command for Adam to "work . . . and keep" the garden (v. 15).

Adam was also to be a *priest*, helping to keep the place where God dwelled holy. God intended for Adam to be a priest-king.

> *Adam's job as king*: subdue and rule over new territory.
> *Adam's job as priest*: keep the garden, where God dwells, holy.

Of course, Adam failed at this job. He let the serpent inside. Noah, Abraham, and the nation of Israel failed, too. Christ then came and perfectly fulfilled the job of priest and king, and then assigned us the job of being priest-kings, too. "You are . . . a royal priesthood" (1 Pet. 2:9).

Here's what's remarkable: your job as a church member is Adam's original job, only it's a new covenant version of it given to you by Christ. We're to push back the borders of the garden like kings while simultaneously watching over the garden like priests.

As kings, we strive to make disciples and be ambassadors of reconciliation. Our goal is to bring more hearts into subjugation to God, more of the earth under the gospel's dominion. We'll think about this further in chapter 8 on the Great Commission (Matt. 28:18–20; 2 Cor. 5:18–20).

> *Our kingly job as members*:
> make disciples, enlarging the kingdom.
>
> *Our priestly job as members*: maintain our holiness by guarding the what and who of the gospel, protecting the kingdom.

As priests, our job is to watch over the place where God dwells, the church. We're to keep holiness separated from unholiness in our individual and corporate lives by attending to the *what* and the *who* of the gospel. In a congregational church, that means you help to make decisions about who is a member and who is not. In every church, that means you help your fellow members walk in holiness and do all you can to make sure your church remains fixed on the gospel (Acts 17:11). We'll think about this further in the next chapter on church discipline (1 Cor. 3:16–17; 2 Cor. 6:14–7:1).

The big takeaway for you right now is that church membership is not a passive thing. It's not just a status. It's not like membership in a country club, a shopper's club, or a gas station rewards program. It's a job where you go to work. You need to get job training. You need to engage it with your mind and heart. You need to think about making an impact. What are you going to produce this week? Are you benefiting the whole team and carrying your weight or are you slacking off?

Furthermore, if your job is to watch over the *what* and *who* of the gospel, you need to study and understand the gospel. What are its implications? What threatens it? How does it relate to other doctrines of the faith, such as the Trinity, sin, or the end times? What does it mean for your work, engaging in politics, or raising children? What does true belief look like in someone's life versus nominal, fake belief? Can you tell the difference between a church member who stumbles into sin because he or she is weak versus a member who pursues sin because he or she is wicked—a wolf in sheep's clothing? Do you know how to respond to both kinds? Can you tell the difference between a true and a false teacher?

Also, do you know other members of your church and invest your life in theirs? Do you let them inconvenience your schedule? Do you help them financially when they're struggling? Or do you basically keep to yourself all week, counting your church involvement as the ninety minutes you show up on Sunday?

We spend years in school and sometimes college, training for our careers. We spend forty hours a week pouring ourselves into them, and we're always learning, training, and growing. All this is good. Yet what might it look like to be similarly focused, deliberate, and hard-working in our job of protecting God's gospel people and extending the gospel's dominion?

A Serious Undertaking

When someone wants to join the church where I pastor, I'll say something like this at the end of the membership interview:

> Friend, by joining this church, you will become jointly responsible for whether or not this congregation continues to faithfully proclaim the gospel. That means you will become jointly responsible both for what this church teaches and for whether or not its members' lives remain faithful. And one day you will stand before God and give an account for how you fulfilled this responsibility. We need more hands for the harvest, so we hope you'll join us in that work.

The membership interview is a kind of job interview. Jesus asked Peter who he thought Jesus was before putting him to work building his church. We should do the same: make sure people know who Jesus is and that they know what job they're undertaking by joining the church.

Recommended Reading

Leeman, Jonathan. *Church Membership: How the World Knows Who Represents Jesus*. Wheaton, IL: Crossway, 2012.

McCracken, Brett. *Uncomfortable: The Awkward and Essential Challenge of Christian Community*. Wheaton, IL: Crossway, 2017.

A church is a group of Christians

↓

who assemble as an earthly embassy
of Christ's heavenly kingdom

↓

to proclaim the good news and
commands of Christ the King;

↓

to affirm one another as his
citizens through the ordinances;

↓

**and to display God's
own holiness and love**

↓

through a unified and
diverse people

↓

in all the world,

↓

following the teaching
and example of elders.

6

Is Church Discipline
Really Loving?

Jonathan Leeman

THE TERM "CHURCH DISCIPLINE" might startle you. *Do churches actually do discipline?* you wonder. *And could discipline possibly be loving?*

Church discipline is, in fact, an essential part of Christian discipleship. Notice how *disciple* and *discipline* are related words. If discipling involves teaching *and* correcting, people typically use the word "discipline" to refer to the corrective half. Both instruction and correction are necessary for growth. How well would students grow with a math teacher who explained the lesson but never corrected their errors? Or a golf instructor who demonstrated how to swing a club but offered no feedback when they kept shanking it?

In the same way, making Christian disciples involves teaching and correcting, and people use the term "church discipline" to mean the second part—*correcting sin.* The discipline process begins with private warnings, as when a friend sat me down on a bench in a church hallway and said, "You can be really selfish," and then listed several concrete examples. That wasn't easy to hear, but my friend was right, and she helped me to grow by speaking plainly. The process ends either when a person repents or, if necessary, when the church removes the unrepentant person from church membership and participation in the Lord's Table.

People will also use this term "church discipline" to refer more narrowly to just this last step, as when they say, "We disciplined Joe from the church." They mean they removed Joe from membership in the church and participation in the Table. They might also use the word *excommunication* (think "ex-communion") to refer to this final step.

Church discipline at this last stage is the flip side of church membership. Remember from the last chapter: membership involves *affirming* a profession of faith. Discipline, in its final stage, means *removing* that affirmation because of a sin that is (1) unrepented, (2) verifiable, and (3) significant. A church isn't declaring with all certainty that someone is a non-Christian when it removes him or her from membership. Churches don't have Holy Spirit X-ray-vision eyes that can see someone's heart. Instead, a church is saying, "We are no longer willing to publicly affirm your profession of faith. That particular sin in your life, which you refuse to let go of [criteria 1] and about which the facts are not in dispute [criteria 2], is significant enough [criteria 3] to undermine the credibility of your profession."

How significant is significant? It requires a case-by-case judgment, to be sure, but the baseline is that some unrepented sins make a profession of faith not credible or unbelievable while others don't. A church probably shouldn't excommunicate a husband who selfishly eats all of the ice cream in the house in spite of his wife's tender remonstrations—a *purely* hypothetical example, to be sure. Yet it should excommunicate a husband who abandons his wife.

Ordinarily, someone disciplined out of a church should remain free to attend the church's public gatherings (unless physical, civil, or other kinds of threats are in play). But he or she is no longer counted as a member. He or she should no longer take the Lord's Supper. Hallway conversations after the service, if there are any, shouldn't be casual and easy. They should be marked by sobriety and earnest calls to repentance.

Church discipline isn't about punishment or retribution any more than a failing grade in a classroom is. The point of discipline, like a failing grade, is to push people toward repentance. As Paul says, "Deliver this man to Satan for the destruction of the flesh, so that his spirit may be saved in the day of the Lord" (1 Cor. 5:5).

Yet beyond the good that church discipline does for the individual in sin, it does good for the church as a whole, particularly for those who might be vulnerable to being taken advantage of by others. In recent years, some people have abandoned churches due to the carelessness of their churches toward abuse. Just be careful not to drop discipline merely because some have done it poorly. Instead, help your church move toward a biblical vision of the church, where abuse has a harder time hiding and vulnerable members find the congregation's fellowship the safest place of all. Such a biblical vision includes a culture of discipling and discipline, where members live openly and transparently, knowing they can confess sins early on when those sins are comparatively "small"—before moral cracks widen to become chasms. Such a church also has a familiar and open process for addressing the "bigger" sins when they do happen, up to and including public announcement and exclusion.

Love in the World's Understanding

That's a quick summary of church discipline. We now want to spend the rest of this chapter placing church discipline into a larger conversation about love. Discipline is hard for us today because it feels unloving to us.

My first experience with church discipline was in the late 1990s, when I was single. I was enjoying lunch with a running partner and good friend. We were discussing my dating life. Then I asked him about his own interests, and he admitted to engaging in a lifestyle of sin. When I asked him if he knew what the Bible taught, he said yes. But he was convinced the Bible was wrong. He refused to turn back. A few days later, I brought another good friend along to confront him again, but we met the same result. Eventually, the church's elders became involved. They received the same response. Finally, the elders presented the case to the church. The church gave my friend an additional two months to repent. He didn't. And so the church decided to remove him from membership as an act of discipline. His sin met all three criteria: he was *unrepentant*; the sin was *verifiable*, meaning everyone agreed on the facts; and it was *significant* enough to undermine the credibility of his profession.

Throughout those months, I sometimes wondered if we were being loving. Carrying out church discipline didn't always *feel* loving. Cultural instincts whispered in my ears that it wasn't.

Our world understands love to be the fire you feel when you meet the person designed for you by the universe or by God. It "happens" when you discover the person who "completes" you. Love is also allowing someone else to pursue his or her own fire, no matter what it is.

Finding love, therefore, depends on knowing yourself, expressing yourself, actualizing yourself. If love requires you to cast off your parents, your class, the church, traditional views of morality, and even society as a whole, so be it. Love requires you to do what's right for you.

Love never judges, we say. Love sets people free. It's the final trump card, the argument to end all arguments, the ultimate justification for doing whatever you most want to do. "But I love it . . ." "If they really love each other, then of course we should accept . . ." "If God is loving, then surely he wouldn't . . ."

Love, or at least our definition of it, is the one nonnegotiable law. The world doesn't believe that God is love, but that love is god.

Sadly, it's not just the culture "out there" that defines love this way. Far too often, Christians succumb to this understanding of love.

To help you rediscover church, we want to persuade you of three further things in this chapter. First, church discipline is biblical. Second, it is loving. While a church might not practice discipline in a loving way, the practice established by Jesus certainly is loving. Third, most remarkably of all, it teaches us about the holy love of God.

We'll conclude by thinking practically about what all this means for you.

Is Discipline Really Biblical?

First, is church discipline really in the Bible? Yes.

Matthew 18. Jesus raises the topic in Matthew 18 while teaching about how a good shepherd will leave the ninety-nine sheep in the flock to pursue the one stray (vv. 10–14). How do we pursue the one stray? Jesus answers:

> If your brother sins against you, go and tell him his fault, between you and him alone. If he listens to you, you have gained your brother. But if he does not listen, take one or two others along with you, that every charge may be established by the evidence of two or three witnesses. If he refuses to listen to them, tell it to the church. And if he refuses to listen even to the church, let him be to you as a Gentile and a tax collector. (vv. 15–17)

Notice Jesus wants to keep the matter as small as possible. But he's also willing to take a matter to the whole church. We all share in that mutual affirmation because we share a family name. We're responsible for one another, like different parts of the body.

Notice also that Jesus believes in due process. A matter must be established by two or three witnesses, as in an Old Testament court of law (Deut. 19:15). He doesn't want false charges or mob justice to rule the church. He doesn't want pastors offering their interpretations of people's character: "He's proud." Instead, sin must be verifiable, the facts not in dispute.

1 Corinthians 5. Paul teaches the same thing in 1 Corinthians 5. He confronts the Corinthian church about a member who's sleeping with his father's wife (v. 1). The church already knows about the situation, but for some reason they're proud. Perhaps they think they're being loving and tolerant. Whatever the case,

Paul says they shouldn't be proud; rather, the man who has done this should be "removed from among you" (v. 2).

What do we take from the fact that Paul's process is much quicker than Jesus's? There's no one-size-fits-all process for church discipline. Each one needs to be handled carefully and wisely, with attention given to the particular facts of the case and any relevant background details. It's not enough for a church to be loving. It must also be wise.

First Corinthians 5 also helps us to see the purpose of discipline. First, discipline exposes sin (see v. 2), which, like cancer, loves to disguise itself.

Second, discipline warns of a greater judgment to come (v. 5).

Third, discipline rescues. It's the church's last resort when every other warning has been ignored (v. 5).

Fourth, discipline protects other church members. Just as cancer spreads from one cell to another, so sin quickly spreads from one person to another (v. 6).

Fifth, discipline preserves the church's witness when it begins to follow in the ways of the world (see v. 1). After all, churches are to be salt and light. "But if salt has lost its taste," Jesus said, "it is no longer good for anything except to be thrown out and trampled under people's feet" (Matt. 5:13).

Church Discipline Teaches Us about God's Love

We can be convinced in our heads that Jesus gave us church discipline, but we might still be afraid to follow his teaching because other instincts tell us discipline is unloving. It's almost as if we think we're more loving than Jesus.

We need to reshape those instincts. So let's ask: Is church discipline really loving?

Clearly the Scriptures connect discipline and love: "The Lord disciplines the one he loves" (Heb. 12:6). God doesn't regard love and discipline as being at odds, but teaches that love motivates discipline.

The author of Hebrews describes discipline as loving because it helps us grow in holiness, righteousness, and peace: "God disciplines us for our good, in order that we may share his holiness. No discipline seems pleasant at the time, but painful. Later on, however, it produces a harvest of righteousness and peace for those who have been trained by it" (Heb. 12:10–11 NIV). The phrase "harvest of righteousness and peace" makes us think of golden fields of wheat. Doesn't that sound like a beautiful picture?

In fact, the Bible says a number of things that don't jibe with our *love = self-expression* culture. It says love doesn't delight in evil but rejoices in the truth (1 Cor. 13:6). And it describes love as a partner with the truth (2 John 1–3). You can say you're loving, but if you're not walking according to truth but are taking delight in what God calls evil, apparently you're not as loving as you think you are.

Jesus himself ties love to keeping God's commandments. He says of himself, "I do as the Father has commanded me, so that the world may know that I love the Father" (John 14:31). He says the same about us: "Whoever has my commandments and keeps them, he it is who loves me" (v. 21). He even tells us that if we keep his commandments, we will abide in his love (15:10). And John says that if we keep God's Word, God's love will be perfected in us (1 John 2:5).

Based on passages such as these, it seems that most of us need a radical reorientation in our understanding of love. In the Bible, love (like faith) leads to obedience, and obedience is a sign of love (and faith), as is shown here:

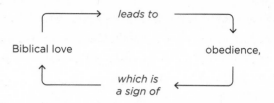

Think about the biblical lesson that "God is love" (1 John 4:16). When people who claim to love God walk away from God, we love them most by correcting them and saying, "No, no, no. God is love. So if you want love, you must return to God." Those who oppose and disobey God are running away from love. They are choosing something besides love, even if they call it love.

If God is love, we love people by sharing the gospel with them so that they might know God.

If God is love, we love people by teaching them everything God commands so that they might image God.

If God is love, we love people by correcting them when they walk away from God.

If God is love, we even love people by removing them from membership in the church when they insist on their own desires more than God's, because their only hope of life and love is to recognize that they are cutting themselves off from God.

Fundamentally, then, churches should practice church discipline for love's sake:

- love for the sinner's sake, that he or she might come to repentance;
- love for the other church members' sake, that they might not be led astray;

- love for the non-Christian neighbors' sake, that they might not just see more worldliness in the church; and
- love for Christ's sake, that we might represent his name rightly.

God's Holy Love

There's one specific thing about God's love that church discipline teaches us, and it is so often missing from definitions: God's love is holy. You can't have God's love apart from his holiness. His love serves his holy purposes, and his holy purposes are loving. Sometimes people pit so-called "holiness churches" against "loving churches." That's impossible. A church must be both of those or it is neither of them.

The relationship between love and holiness also helps us understand the Bible's long-running theme of exclusion and exile. Passages such as Matthew 18 and 1 Corinthians 5 don't offer us pictures of God doing something new or different. They present us a quick glimpse of what God has always done. He has always removed sin from his presence. God excluded Adam and Eve from the garden when they sinned. He excluded the fallen world from Noah's ark. He excluded the Canaanites from the promised land, and eventually he excluded his own people from the land, too. All the laws for the tabernacle also worked to exclude things that were unclean and unholy. And on the last day, God promises to exclude all whose faith doesn't rest in the finished work of Christ's incarnate life, substitutionary death, and death-defeating resurrection.

Yet there's a flip side. Even as God has excluded sin and sinners, he has simultaneously drawn people to himself for the purpose of refashioning them in his image so that they might display his holy love to the nations—so that "the earth will be filled / with the knowledge of the glory of the LORD / as the waters cover the sea" (Hab. 2:14). How will the earth be so filled? Think back to God's command to Adam and Eve to fill the earth: his image bearers, having been born again by the Spirit, would fulfill that original mandate and display his loving, holy, and righteous image everywhere.

Our congregations, like pins spread across a map, are the start of this. They are the embassies of God's glorious, holy love. God's very purpose for the church, Paul tells us, is that "through the church the manifold wisdom of God might now be made known to the rulers and authorities in the heavenly places" (Eph. 3:10). To this end, Paul then prays that we would have the power "to comprehend with all the saints what is the breadth and length and height and depth, and to know the love of Christ that surpasses knowledge" (vv. 18–19). Displaying God's wisdom and glory means knowing and experiencing Christ's love—its width, length, height, and depth.

What This Means for You

There is still more to learn about church discipline. When does restoration occur? (When there's repentance.) How does a church practice discipline? (By involving as few people as possible, by giving individuals the benefit of the doubt, by letting church leaders guide the process, by eventually involving the whole church, and more.) We just wanted you to dip your toe in the water.

In the final analysis, church discipline is tough, but loving. It protects people from self-deception. One time, my wife and I had to confront a close friend of ours over a sinful decision she was making in the workplace. She rejected our correction. We involved two more friends, and then two more. Each time she rebuffed our love. At several points through this process, which lasted a few weeks, I had an upset stomach and could not sleep—and neither of these things is normal for me. Yet we pressed ahead because we believed that God is more loving and wise than we are, and we could trust his Word. Wonderfully, this woman eventually came back to us and told us that she had renounced the sinful work decision. Praise God! It was tough, but worth it.

Yet beyond protecting people from self-deception, church discipline also protects the vulnerable from those who would prey on them. Readers may recall the #MeToo movement from 2018, which gave a voice to victims of sexual assault. The label #Church-Too quickly followed. More and more voices began calling upon churches to address their own sinful neglect. If abuse is terrible, a church that ignores it is at least as bad, precisely because God has commissioned churches to be places of redress, remedy, and restoration for all the injustices the world throws at us, including abuse and assault. That call, no doubt, was salutary and good for churches to hear. Thankfully, many churches have a track record of faithfully addressing these matters decisively and quickly. Others do not. They remain undereducated, ill-equipped, and slow to respond. Or, worse, they refuse to see the problem. Either way, moving forward, the solution is not to abandon churches. It's to make sure our churches are opening the Bible and grabbing hold of the very tool God has provided to (at best) prevent or (at worst) guide a response to abuse: a culture of discipleship and discipline. A church that practices discipline in a humble, loving, and responsible fashion should never need a #MeToo or #ChurchToo movement in the first place.

What's the takeaway in all of this for you? Make sure you're building relationships with other members of the church so that you can know them and they can know you. Trust grows in an environment of conversational humility and honesty. Work to be the kind of person who is easy to correct. If you're not, your friends and family members will quickly learn that correcting you is a futile, even dangerous exercise, and they'll stop. How unprotected that will leave you!

Invite people to know you. Invite critical feedback. Confess sin. Risk embarrassment. Encourage others in their walk with Christ. Be willing to have those awkward conversations in which you gently, tenderly challenge sin. Typically, this means starting with questions, not accusations, in order to make sure you understand correctly.

All this is not just the pastor's job but every member's job. When you and the other members of your church live this way, the vast majority of discipline in a church will never travel beyond two or three people. The elders will never hear of it. The body will be working as it should, each part building up the body in love (Eph. 4:15–16). And little by little, from one degree of glory to the next, your congregation will become an embassy that displays the holy love of God.

Recommended Reading

Leeman, Jonathan. *Understanding Church Discipline.* Nashville: B&H, 2016.

Leeman, Jonathan. *The Rule of Love: How the Local Church Should Reflect God's Love and Authority.* Wheaton, IL: Crossway, 2018.

A church is a group of Christians

↓

who assemble as an earthly embassy
of Christ's heavenly kingdom

↓

to proclaim the good news and
commands of Christ the King;

↓

to affirm one another as his
citizens through the ordinances;

↓

and to display God's
own holiness and love

↓

**through a unified and
diverse people**

↓

in all the world,

↓

following the teaching
and example of elders.

7

How Do I Love Members Who Are Different?

Collin Hansen

IMAGINE THAT YOUR GOAL is to build a church as quickly as possible. Your main objective is numeric growth. You want to attract people. What's your strategy?

You'd probably start with teaching, right? These days you can develop a global following through books, podcasts, and videos. You might even conclude that online or virtual church is the best way to quickly increase your numbers. Building around one dynamic teaching personality is probably the fastest way to grow a large church.

But it's not the only way. Consider the music. Lots of churches are still stuck in the past with their so-called worship experience. So you decide that your church will perform only the latest, cutting-edge music. You'll hire a staff of twentysomething musicians and even encourage them to record their music for digital release. That way your church can generate an online fan base that will hopefully add to your church's reputation for innovation and growth.

What about community? People say they want music and teaching, but what they really need are friends. That's not easy to facilitate when everyone's so busy with work and travel. Still, small groups appear to be the most effective way to help people get to know one another. But how will you organize them? You could gather people according to geography. Some preexisting groups of friends could be accommodated. Probably the best approach, however, is to organize by stage of life or interests. Put all the first-time parents together. Put all the singles together in one group and the empty nesters in another. Start a group for people who enjoy riding motorcycles. Start another for knitters. The possibilities are endless. Eventually people will be attracted to your church for the variety of programs you offer. You'll have the best youth ministry in town, so parents will switch churches. Start a Saturday night service so that men who enjoy golf can free up their Sunday mornings. The more different ways people can participate in your church without needing to change their lifestyle, the easier it will be for your church to grow.

This exercise gives you a window into how many church leaders today think. We started with the stated goal of numeric growth. But did you catch the underlying assumption in all of these strategies? People like to be around people like themselves. They feel comfortable in familiar, predictable patterns. They want to be with people who enjoy the same teaching style, have the same musical preferences, and ask the same questions about marriage, parenting, or dating—and, often, have the same skin color. The quickest, most efficient way to build a large church is to identify a segment of the population that shares a set of interests and cater to them in how you teach, sing, and foster friendships. This isn't a new trend. It's simply been assumed in much of church history.

That's why we need to rediscover the church as the fellowship of differents. The local congregation is where Jesus teaches us to love all kinds of people, even our enemies—one tribe and another, one race and another, one nation and another. And like the morning sun peeking over the horizon, so the fulfillment of the Old Testament prophecy should begin in our fellowships:

> They shall beat their swords into plowshares,
>   and their spears into pruning hooks;
> nation shall not lift up sword against nation,
>   neither shall they learn war anymore. (Isa. 2:4)

So look around the Sunday afternoon potluck table, the Wednesday night small-group trip to the nursing home, or the Friday morning men's prayer group and ask what you're seeing. Is it love shared between a unified diversity of people?

Church for Sinners

From the outside, Jesus's twelve disciples look largely the same: Jewish men. Several of them worked as fishermen before Jesus called them to follow him. With others, we're never told their vocation. But we know that Jesus called Matthew while he was sitting at a toll booth (Matt. 9:9). We might not think much about that detail, but Matthew knew it was important for his Jewish readers. Why? Because they hated tax collectors—not in the way folks might resent the IRS, but much worse. Jewish tax collectors worked for a hated occupying force. They collected money that fed and supplied the very Roman soldiers who ruled them with brutal efficiency. Because Jesus called Matthew, he angered the Pharisees: "Why does your teacher eat with tax collectors and sinners?" they asked Jesus's disciples. Jesus overheard their question and answered: "Those who are well have no need of a physician, but those who are sick. Go and learn what this means: 'I desire mercy, and not sacrifice.' For I came not to call the righteous, but sinners" (Matt. 9:11–13).

Many today, both inside and outside the church, share the Pharisees' confusion. Isn't church for people with the right politics? Isn't church for people who have their act together? Isn't church for people who look, think, and talk like I do?

To a visitor who's unfamiliar with church, everyone else can look so happy, so successful, so put together. And sometimes that's exactly the impression the church wants to leave.

But it's not what Jesus intended. Only the sick go to the doctor. And only the sinners go to church. The Pharisees thought they were righteous apart from Jesus. They didn't need him. Yet Matthew and the other sinners knew they needed Jesus. They were ashamed of their past, guilt-ridden over what they had done and not done. His love was unlike anything they'd experienced before. Once they were outcasts. Now they had been brought near to the Son of God! They couldn't live without him.

These tax collectors and sinners would not have shared fellowship apart from Jesus. They did not have much in common, except the rejection of the Pharisees. But Jesus brought together people who wouldn't have been natural friends and allies. In the same group of twelve disciples Jesus also called a man named Simon, whom everyone knew as the Zealot (Acts 1:13). The zealot party worked to violently overthrow the Roman occupiers. They resented the Pharisees for not doing enough to expel the foreigners. But they really hated collaborators—men like Matthew the tax collector.

You can imagine the awkward campfire conversations between Simon and Matthew. Yet Jesus called them both. He loved them both. He devoted years of his life to teaching both of them about the kingdom of God that transcends all earthly divisions.

Negative Community

The reason we need to rediscover the church as a fellowship of differents is because we too easily fall into the world's ideas about community. The world gives us two options. One perspective asks us to celebrate diversity by prioritizing differences in ethnicity, nationality, gender, and, increasingly, sexual orientation. This perspective trains us to feel right and good when these various identities are included in our community. A room full of faces of the same color feels wrong, even immoral.

A second perspective asks us to celebrate uniformity. In much of the world, you can't—or at least aren't supposed to—mix different ethnicities. You might live in a remote territory with only one economic class or ethnicity. Or in a country that practices a caste system that separates people before they're born, with no possibility of changing positions. Or in a political system that demands obedience to the state in all things, including religion. Uniformity is considered the highest value. A room where people disagree with each other over politics or their view of the world feels wrong, even immoral.

At first, these two perspectives—diversity and uniformity—might appear to be pushing in opposite directions. But these differences obscure the underlying similarities. Both perspectives create community through exclusion. It's more obvious in the uniformity perspective. If you put out the wrong yard sign, don't go to the right church, or associate with people from the wrong caste, you're excluded from the community. The same thing happens, though, in the push toward diversity. Only a certain kind of diversity is allowed. You can be from a different ethnicity, but you cannot disagree on sexual ethics. You can be proud to come from another country, but you cannot support the wrong political party. You can be celebrated for your gender, but not for insisting on biological differences between the genders.

Whatever their pretenses, both perspectives create community through exclusion. They're like fraternities or sororities, which build community by creating an exclusive club. You can enter only by permission. The same goes for a country club or a neighborhood that filters out undesirable elements by income level. Or for a protest march that brooks no protest from within. Or for an academic program that snuffs out free inquiry and ideological dissent. You're in because others are out.

How to Get Noticed by the World

Our churches sometimes take on this posture, whether by prizing uniformity or diversity, because this is what we know about community. We don't know how to have a church where people can disagree about politics because we try not to associate with anyone who makes us uncomfortable. We don't know how to build a multiethnic church because we don't live multiethnic lives. We don't know how to include different economic classes because they can't be found in our neighborhoods. We don't know how to prioritize our shared unity in Christ because we're accustomed to observing our physical differences.

When a church follows these patterns of the world, it does not get noticed by the world. Why? Because the members don't need the church for this kind of community. You can join a protest march or political party if you want shared ideological zeal. You can join a sports team or gaming community if you need friends to pass the time. You can join the old-timers at the cafe down the street if you want to gripe about the weather and your aches and pains. The church that gets noticed by the world brings together people who don't normally associate—the tax collectors and zealots, the sinners and Pharisees. That's what made the early church so strange that some said it had turned the world upside down (Acts 17:6).

In the ancient world, religion was tied up with other identities, especially people's politics and ethnicities or tribes. When they went to war, they fought against people with different local gods and different rulers. The Romans conquered smaller groups like this all over the known world. The Jews were strange to them in insisting on one God instead of many. But they didn't stop the temple worship of this God until the Jews revolted against Rome's political authority.

The Christians were different. They worshiped this same God. But they also worshiped a man, Jesus, who claimed to be God. Strangely, the Christians also insisted that he was not some local teacher or political revolutionary, but the Lord of the universe. And while Jesus submitted to local authorities, he also claimed that they had no authority except what he had granted to them. No one had ever seen or heard anything like it. Christianity, then, was uniquely appealing to people across the Roman Empire because Jesus brought together the people who didn't normally associate—slaves and free people, poor and wealthy, Jews and Gentiles. This unified diversity also made Christianity uniquely threatening to the political powers in Rome, who rightly saw their authority subverted by the values of a higher kingdom.

This kind of community, this fellowship of differents united by Christ alone, is what we need to rediscover in the church. And it's the kind of community that gets noticed by the world. It's the kind of community that threatens the world's status quo. This community is built on common love and belief in Jesus Christ. As the apostle Paul urged the Ephesians,

> Walk in a manner worthy of the calling to which you have been called, with all humility and gentleness, with patience, bearing with one another in love, eager to maintain the unity of the Spirit in the bond of peace. There is one body and one Spirit— just as you were called to the one hope that belongs to your call—one Lord, one faith, one baptism, one God and Father of all, who is over all and through all and in all. (Eph. 4:1–6)

No pandemic, election, or viral video can threaten this kind of unity. When controversy hits, this church community draws closer together in love, empathy, and trust. Its members are "eager to maintain the unity of the Spirit in the bond of peace."

Withstanding Division

At the same time, this community can withstand worldly divisions because its members value and respect their differences. The apostle Paul labored to correct the church in Corinth as it struggled to find unity amid difference. The church's divisions inspired his famous teaching about love: "Love bears all things, believes all things, hopes all things, endures all things" (1 Cor. 13:7).

Their divisions also drew out his clearest teaching on the body of Christ. He used this metaphor to explain how the church needs all its members working together. In a body, the foot doesn't look down on the hand. The ear isn't jealous of the eye because you need to hear as much as you need to see. Anyone can relate to the experience of how much pain and discomfort can come from a body part you didn't think much about. That's why, Paul said, we can never take for granted the so-called lesser parts of the body. "God has so composed the body, giving greater honor to the part that lacked it, that there may be no division in the body, but that the members may have the same care for one another. If one member suffers, all suffer together; if one member is honored, all rejoice together" (1 Cor. 12:24–26).

More Durable Church

The body is a fellowship of differents. We are not alike, and we need each other. We have not been gifted the same way, and that's how God intended it for our good. We confess the same belief in Jesus Christ, but we enjoy a diversity of experiences. This is God's vision for the church that we must rediscover. This model does not offer the fastest way to build the largest church. But it's the most durable way to build a healthy church.

If you want to build a large church quickly, you'll center on the pastor's unique personality and teaching instead of the various gifts God has given to every member of the body. You will also select music that appeals to your preferred age, class, and ethnic demographic (for example, white twentysomething professionals with disposable income and abundant time and need for community).

It's not that such churches are wrong and sinful. In fact, many if not most churches in world history generally pulled from the same kinds of people with the same kinds of interests. In some cases, as with ethnic minorities in the United States, they built separate churches because they were excluded from established churches, either because of racism or simple language barriers. Indeed, God seems to employ many different kinds of churches together in order to reach the same community with the good news about Jesus.

But the example of Jesus's disciples and the early churches led by Paul suggest something we need to rediscover today. Politics and pandemic have stressed many congregations past the breaking point. It might seem easier to look for a church where everyone thinks, votes, and sins the same way you do. It's better for your spiritual growth, however, to hunker down in a fellowship of differents.

To honor people whose abilities differ from yours.

To hope all things in love.

To maintain the unity of the Spirit in the bond of peace.

To respect the zealot or tax collector sitting next to you.

You want to find a church that grabs this world's attention? Find a church that looks like the world to come.

Recommended Reading

Dever, Mark, and Jamie Dunlop. *The Compelling Community: Where God's Power Makes a Church Attractive*. Wheaton, IL: Crossway, 2015.

Ince, Irwyn L., Jr. *The Beautiful Community: Unity, Diversity, and the Church at Its Best*. Downers Grove, IL: InterVarsity Press, 2020.

A church is a group of Christians

↓

who assemble as an earthly embassy
of Christ's heavenly kingdom

↓

to proclaim the good news and
commands of Christ the King;

↓

to affirm one another as his
citizens through the ordinances;

↓

and to display God's
own holiness and love

↓

through a unified and
diverse people

↓

in all the world,

↓

following the teaching
and example of elders.

8

How Do We Love Outsiders?

Collin Hansen

WHAT IS A CHURCH FOR? What is supposed to happen in all of the church's youth programs, worship services, Bible studies, and small groups? How are you supposed to feel, and what are you supposed to do, as part of a church?

Maybe the answers to those questions are obvious to you. But throughout history, churches have answered those questions in at least four different ways. We can compare these four alternatives to what we find in God's Word about what the church should do for people outside its walls and also for the people inside. Some of these answers will overlap; they're not necessarily mutually exclusive. Yet churches typically emphasize just one of these aspects of the relationship between insiders and outsiders.

First, some believe that church is for evangelism. Church aims to get people inside a building on Sunday morning so they can hear the good news about Jesus and be converted. Preaching and

teaching stay focused on the basics: our problem with sin, the sacrifice of Jesus, and the necessity of belief. Worship services tend to
cycle through standard series on relationships, parenting, finances,
pop culture, and other topics that connect with outsiders. The
teacher aims to connect these life situations to our need for Jesus.

Second, some believe that church is for good works. Church
aims to mobilize the people inside to help people on the outside in
tangible ways. These churches operate soup kitchens and second-
hand clothing stores. They run job programs for ex-convicts and
English language classes for immigrants and refugees. Preaching
and teaching emphasize Jesus's good works and his commandment
to love our neighbors as ourselves. Leaders exhort the insiders
to work and vote for change that will benefit the less fortunate
outside. Worship services feature announcements about work
days and the need for volunteers. They also highlight reports of
outsiders whose lives have been helped by insiders.

Third, some believe that church is for healing. Church aims
to show outsiders that life gets better when they come inside the
church. Preaching and teaching stress the miracles of Jesus and the
power of the Spirit, and how he gives us the same means to heal
people of their physical, spiritual, financial, and mental suffering
today. Sermons stress that insiders can overcome any challenge
with the help of God. Worship services feature uplifting music
and bodily responses to the Spirit's moving. Some services might
concentrate almost exclusively on prayer for immediate healing.

Fourth, some believe that church is for dispensing grace.
Church aims to give insiders the forgiveness they cannot receive
apart from the church. Preaching and teaching focus on the
church's role as mediator between humans and God. Worship

services culminate with insiders receiving from the leader the body and blood of Christ as bread and wine. An outsider to this particular congregation might be an insider at a different congregation, but will recognize many similarities no matter which service he or she attends in this kind of church.

Perhaps you recognize your current church in one of these scenarios. You might see some of two or three churches that you know. Or maybe you're so new to church that they're all equally unfamiliar! You might visit one church as an outsider and feel as if everything has been planned just for your benefit. In another church, no one may even notice you. In this chapter, then, we aim to help you rediscover church by exploring what the Bible teaches about the purpose of church and how insiders and outsiders should relate.

Great Commission

We start with the final words of Jesus to his disciples before he ascended to heaven, after his resurrection:

> All authority in heaven and on earth has been given to me. Go therefore and make disciples of all nations, baptizing them in the name of the Father and of the Son and of the Holy Spirit, teaching them to observe all that I have commanded you. And behold, I am with you always, to the end of the age. (Matt. 28:18–20)

Jesus bookended this parting message by explaining himself. All authority belongs to him, so his command is binding. The disciples did not have the authority to do whatever they wanted.

Jesus had promised that he would build his church. Only he has the proper authority. Jesus also promised that no matter what might befall his disciples, he would be with them. But not just to the end of their lives. This promise and command apply to all disciples to come, to the end of the age.

Considering Jesus gave these words before he ascended into heaven, his commitment must have comforted the disciples, who had little idea what lay in store for them after he left.

Jesus delivered this parting message to the ultimate insiders, the men who had walked and talked with him for years. But it's noteworthy that here he did not say anything about them as insiders. He only commanded what they must do for outsiders. Just as he made them his disciples, they should go and make other disciples. The scope, however, has dramatically changed. Their horizon will expand far beyond the backwater of Galilee and the city of Jerusalem. Jesus sent them to "all nations."

It's remarkable to look back and see how they obeyed and made disciples everywhere from India to Africa to Europe.

What, then, were these insiders supposed to do to turn outsiders into disciples of Jesus? For starters, they baptized. Churches today disagree about whether baptism follows shortly after birth or shortly after profession of faith in Jesus Christ. It's beyond the scope of this short book to settle that dispute. Yet everyone agrees that the disciples baptized new believers in the name of the Father, the Son, and the Holy Spirit, as Jesus commanded. That means they taught outsiders about the Trinity, one God in three persons. Considering Jewish belief about one God, and Roman belief about many gods, this doctrine would have required patient, careful, extended treatment. It would not have been self-evident to the outsiders the disciples encountered, no matter where they traveled.

The last charge from Jesus encompasses just about anything you can imagine: "teaching them to observe all that I have commanded you." We have four books of the Bible full of Jesus's teaching. The disciples had several years with him, too. They could not have fulfilled this command by teaching only about the cross and the empty tomb, then pushing for a decision to believe. Yes, conversion makes outsiders into insiders. But the new insiders then must learn to "observe" Jesus's teaching. And just as Jesus set an example for the disciples, so also the disciples must have taught new believers to observe them and their teaching as they followed Jesus's commands. Again, obeying this aspect of the command we know as the Great Commission would have taken time and patience. It's probably not the kind of thing you can accomplish only over video calls, let alone one-directional podcasts. This kind of teaching is best accomplished in person, in relationship, in dialogue—in church.

Church Today

What can we conclude, then, from the Great Commission about what church is for? How do insiders and outsiders relate? We can see that Jesus asked the first church leaders, the ultimate insiders, to undertake the business of turning outsiders into insiders through conversion. That process could start within their own homes, with their children and extended families, but it would eventually extend to strangers around the world. The church must never lose sight of this evangelistic calling. Whatever else the church does, it teaches and then models how to become a disciple of Jesus Christ.

We can see that a church must build relationships of depth and endurance. It's impossible to teach everything Jesus commanded to people you barely know and hardly see. Compared to previous centuries, furthermore, the difficulty of teaching everything Jesus commanded takes even more time today since, in the West at least, we've returned to a state of religious confusion closer to what the disciples would have encountered. Through the history of Christendom, whether of the European established-church or the American easy-believism variety, outsiders knew how to talk and act like insiders, even if they didn't actually believe in Jesus. They knew the lingo. They observed the holidays. They could identify the three persons of the Trinity as easily as the three branches of American government. We call this Christian nominalism. Yet nominalism is drying up except in shrinking corners of the West.

I talk often with pastors who work with young people. And for the last five years at least, I've heard a consistent message: it takes twice the amount of time to make the same amount of progress in discipleship today as a decade ago. Fewer and fewer outsiders know anything Jesus said beyond generic allusions to judgment and love. When they become insiders, they understand little about what it means to follow Jesus—who he is, what he has done, what he has commanded. The rediscovered church can't afford to repeat the same basic self-help mantras without plumbing any theological depths. Such shallow faith doesn't help new believers obey Jesus given that he told us to expect the world to hate his followers (Matt. 5:11; 10:22; Mark 13:13; Luke 21:17; John 5:18).

A similar word of caution applies to churches that focus on healing or dispensing grace. Prayer should indeed characterize any faithful church. And the Spirit has the power to heal—both insiders and outsiders. But the Spirit's role is to help us remember what Jesus taught and did (John 14:26). Any physical healing or financial help on this side of heaven is good but not ultimate. Your credit card debt may be forgiven on earth. But unless God has forgiven your sins by the blood of Jesus, your debt of sin remains, along with God's eternal judgment. We must be careful not to leave the impression that joining the church brings tangible financial or physical benefits here and now. Otherwise Jesus becomes the means to a worldly and temporary end.

When it comes to dispensing grace, we walk a fine line in the church. This book is about how the body of Christ is essential. God has authorized church leaders on his behalf to administer the ordinances of baptism and the Lord's Supper. They guard these means of grace, which belong only to insiders. You can't just take a dip in the backyard pool and wash down some Wonder Bread with a can of Mountain Dew and call it church.

At the same time, no mere mortal determines your spiritual destiny, whether you're on the outside or inside. The apostle Paul told Timothy, his protégé and the pastor in Ephesus, "For there is one God, and there is one mediator between God and men, the man Christ Jesus, who gave himself as a ransom for all, which is the testimony given at the proper time" (1 Tim. 2:5–6). Grace comes from God to all who ask by faith. It is not held in storage by the church and dispensed at the leaders' behest. You don't need the church to be born again, but you need the church's help to walk on your wobbly legs of fledgling faith.

What about Everything Else Jesus Commanded?

So far in this chapter, we've established that church is for helping outsiders become insiders through conversion. When those outsiders become part of the church, the insiders patiently and diligently teach them to obey everything Jesus commanded. As you rediscover church, you'll find that not everyone excels at doing both. Sometimes you'll hear a lot about the gospel, namely, the cross and the resurrection. But you won't hear as much from the Gospels, those four books based on accounts from Jesus's first disciples. They culminate in the cross and resurrection after dozens of chapters with Jesus's teaching. Understanding the relationship between the gospel and the Gospels is key to rediscovering the church's commitment to both evangelism and to living as members dedicated to good deeds—raising children in the fear of the Lord, going to work every day as unto Christ, doing good to our non-Christian neighbors, pursuing works of compassion and justice, engaging in the public square as we have opportunity, and more.

The very structure of the Gospels tells us that Jesus understood his mission as offering himself as a sacrifice to atone for sin. He explained to the disciples, "For even the Son of Man came not to be served but to serve, and to give his life as a ransom for many" (Mark 10:45; see also Matt. 20:28). Matthew's Gospel hinges on the point when Peter confessed that Jesus is the Christ, the long-promised Messiah of Israel (Matt. 16:16). From this point, Jesus began to explain to his disciples that he would need to go to Jerusalem, suffer at the hands of the Jewish leaders, die on the cross, and rise from the dead on the third day (v. 21). When we understand this mission of Jesus, we can understand the mission of the church to share this gospel about what Jesus has done.

But if that's all Jesus came to do, we wouldn't need all the other chapters in the Gospels. We wouldn't need the Sermon on the

Mount from Matthew 5 to 7. We wouldn't need Jesus to explain how insiders ought to relate to one another, how they should relate to outsiders, and how they contribute to a good and just society. In this sermon, we hear from Jesus, "You are the light of the world. A city set on a hill cannot be hidden. . . . Let your light shine before others, so that they may see your good works and give glory to your Father who is in heaven" (5:14, 16).

This passage holds the key for reconciling evangelism and good works, insiders and outsiders. Have you ever attended a Christmas Eve candlelight service? If not, you can get the basic idea fairly easily. While singing along with "O Holy Night" or another Christmas hymn, each person lights his or her candle and passes the flame to the next person. What starts as a dark room at the beginning of the hymn blazes with light and heat by the end. One candle alight shines bright against the darkness. Dozens of candles alight chase the darkness away.

That's what happens when a church obeys the commands of Jesus together. The commands to forsake anger. To reject lust. To love enemies. To give to the needy. To not be anxious about anything. When Christians inside act this way toward one another and toward outsiders, the world sees their good works as a city set on a hill and illuminated with the twinkling lights of Christmas. Their light shines in such a way that outsiders want to come inside and give glory to the Father in heaven.

Admittedly, the order here is crucial. Too often, Christians and churches become so preoccupied with redeeming the culture or transforming the city that they fail to get their own houses in order. As we've labored to say throughout this book, churches must first seek to become redeemed cultures and transformed heavenly cities. Only then can their love, good works, and pursuit of justice spill outward with integrity. When this happens, the beleaguered citizens of this world and its failed revolutions may then seek refuge through our embassy door.

Good to Everyone

So does the church exist for insiders or outsiders? In complementary ways, both. The apostle Paul taught, "So then, as we have opportunity, let us do good to everyone, and especially to those who are of the household of faith" (Gal. 6:10). Every outsider is welcome in church and invited to become an insider by faith.

Inside the church, Christians learn to obey everything Jesus commanded, including how they should honor God and love outsiders in their families, their work, and their neighborhoods. Together, when insiders do good to one another, they shine as a beacon of holy hope for a world trapped by the darkness of night. Adolphe-Charles Adam puts it well in his lyrics for the Christmas hymn "O Holy Night":

> Truly he taught us to love one another;
> His law is love and his gospel is peace.
> Chains shall he break, for the slave is our brother;
> And in his name all oppression shall cease.

Recommended Reading

Keller, Timothy. *Generous Justice: How God's Grace Makes Us Just*. New York: Viking, 2010.

Stiles, Mack. *Evangelism: How the Whole Church Speaks of Jesus*. Wheaton, IL: Crossway, 2014.

A church is a group of Christians

↓

who assemble as an earthly embassy
of Christ's heavenly kingdom

↓

to proclaim the good news and
commands of Christ the King;

↓

to affirm one another as his
citizens through the ordinances;

↓

and to display God's
own holiness and love

↓

through a unified and
diverse people

↓

in all the world,

↓

**following the teaching
and example of elders.**

9

Who Leads?

Jonathan Leeman

EVERYONE KNOWS WHAT a pastor is, right? Even non-Christians kind of know. If nothing else, they've seen them on television. Pastors lead churches. They stand up front during church services. They talk for a while. Maybe, after the service, they stand in the back by the exit and shake people's hands on their way out the door. Throughout the week, they do other kinds of good stuff. Or something.

Perhaps it would be better to say that most people have a vague impression of what a pastor is. That impression has been formed by experience, whether from watching television or from observing the pastor of the church they occasionally attended as children.

That means that if we start comparing notes, we'll discover that our impressions diverge. Some think of a handsome and charismatic showman, capable of enchanting a room of five thousand with comedian-like timing. Others think of a kindly older man whose sermons ramble and are a little hard to follow because he spent most of the week visiting hospitals or helping neighbors in need. Others see a severe lecturer with furrowed brow, waving his Bible from the pulpit and declaring week after week certain opinions on everything. Still others remember the hurt or even abuse they experienced from the man the congregation esteemed and honored with the title of "the pastor."

Jesus's Discipleship Program

The goal of this book has been to rediscover church, which is why we have spent most of our time on the church—that is, all the members; that is, *you*. Yet the leaders play a crucial role in any church, and we'll refer to them as *pastors* and *elders* interchangeably, because that's what the Bible does (see Acts 20:17, 28; Titus 1:5, 7; 1 Pet. 5:1–2). Your ability to do your job as a church member depends on pastors or elders doing their jobs. Your job, as we saw in chapter 5, is to be a priest-king. Jesus tasked you with watching over the *what* and the *who* of the gospel, as well as extending the gospel's dominion throughout the earth by making disciples. But what is a pastor's job?

As churches emerge from COVID-19, it's as important as ever before that we know the answer to that question because of the impact the COVID-19 quarantines had on trust inside of churches—trust among members and trust toward leaders. We'll think about this more in a moment, but part of building trust back up is knowing exactly what a pastor's job is. The short description of a pastor's job is that he is to equip you to do your job.

We learn this in Ephesians 4:11–16. The apostle Paul tells us that Jesus has given a number of gifts to his church, including pastors (v. 11). Then he tells us why Jesus gave churches this gift: "to equip the saints for the work of ministry, for building up the body of Christ" (v. 12). The pastor's job is to equip the saints to do their job. They teach us how to minister to one another, to this end:

> Speaking the truth in love, we are to grow up in every way into him who is the head, into Christ, from whom the whole body, joined and held together by every joint with which it is equipped, when each part is working properly, makes the body grow so that it builds itself up in love. (vv. 15–16)

Each part of the body has work to do. We all participate in the project of building up the body in love. And pastors teach and train us for this work.

The weekly church gathering, then, is a time of job training. It allows those in the office of pastor to equip those in the office of member to know the gospel, to live by the gospel, to protect the church's gospel witness, and to extend the gospel's reach into one another's lives and among outsiders. If Jesus tasks members with affirming and building up one another in the gospel, he tasks pastors with training them to do this. If the pastors don't do their jobs well, neither will the members.

Elders' job + members' job = Jesus's discipleship program

When you put the pastor's job together with the members' job, what do you get? Jesus's discipleship program. This is not a program you can purchase from a Christian bookstore, a boxed package that comes with a teacher's manual, a student's guide, and posters for the Sunday school classroom wall. It's right there in Ephesians 4.

Equipping by Teaching

A pastor's or elder's ministry of equipping centers on his teaching and his life. We encounter the formula in Paul's instruction to Timothy: "Keep a close watch on yourself and on the teaching. Persist in this, for by so doing you will save both yourself and your hearers" (1 Tim. 4:16).

Let's take each in turn. One of the main things that sets elders apart from members is that they must be "able to teach" (1 Tim. 3:2). That doesn't mean an elder must step into the pulpit, stand in front of a thousand people, and enthrall them with his wisdom and wit. It means that if you're struggling to understand the Bible or how to handle a tough life situation, you know you can stop by his house and ask him for help, and you'll get a biblical answer. You trust that, when he opens the Bible, he doesn't say crazy things from it. He provides you with a faithful understanding of it. He teaches "what accords with sound doctrine" (Titus 2:1).

Some Sunday afternoon, read through the entirety of Paul's three letters to two pastors, Timothy and Titus, and underline every reference to teaching. Your hand might get tired. To pick just one: Paul says in his second letter to Timothy that Timothy must hold on to the pattern of sound teaching that he has heard from Paul (2 Tim. 1:13). What he has heard from Paul he should commit to faithful men, who will be able to teach others also

(2:2). He is to be diligent in correctly teaching the word of truth (v. 15). He is to avoid empty speech that deviates from the truth (vv. 16, 18). And he must teach and instruct only as God would have him teach, knowing that repentance will lead to a knowledge of the truth (vv. 24–25). Paul concludes by commanding Timothy to persist in preaching the Word, correcting, rebuking, and encouraging with great patience (4:2).

The picture Paul provides for both Timothy and Titus is the slow, patient, day-to-day, repetitious work of seeking to grow people in godliness. An elder doesn't force but teaches, because a forced act of godliness is no godliness at all. A godly act is willfully chosen from a regenerate, new covenant heart.

When elders teach, the congregation begins to serve and do good works. A wonderful picture of this pattern occurs in Acts 16, when Paul and his companions show up for the first time in Philippi. Paul teaches a group of women, including one named Lydia. "The Lord opened her heart to pay attention to what was said by Paul," we read (v. 14). He baptizes her. Then she says to Paul and his companions, "If you have judged me to be faithful to the Lord, come to my house and stay." Luke, who is writing this account, concludes, "And she prevailed upon us" (v. 15). So Paul preaches, Lydia gets saved, and then she immediately gets to work showing hospitality!

Equipping by Setting an Example

Elders don't only teach. They also must set an example for the flock in their lives. "I exhort the elders among you," Peter teaches, "shepherd the flock of God that is among you" (1 Pet. 5:1–2). How do they do that, Peter? By "being examples," he answers (v. 3).

An elder works by calling people to imitate his ways. So says Paul to the Corinthians: "I urge you, then, be imitators of me. That is why I sent you Timothy, my beloved and faithful child in the Lord, to remind you of my ways in Christ, as I teach them everywhere in every church" (1 Cor. 4:16–17).

Sometimes Christians are surprised when they search for an elder's job description in the Bible, only to discover that the authors are more systematic in describing an elder's *character* (1 Tim. 3:2–7; Titus 1:6–9). Also interesting is the fact that these descriptions of an elder's character point to attributes that should characterize every Christian—being sober-minded, self-controlled, respectable, hospitable, not a drunkard, not violent but gentle, not quarrelsome, not a lover of money, and so forth. Shouldn't every Christian aspire to those things? The only exceptions are "able to teach" (1 Tim. 3:2) and "not a recent convert" (v. 6). Folks might wonder why Paul doesn't require, well, something more extraordinary of elders, such as "demonstrated track record in leading large organizations," "started seven orphanages," or "spearheaded a revival leading to the conversion of hundreds." The reason, it would seem, takes us right back to the idea of an elder being an example. Other than being able to teach, his life should be something that other Christians can copy.

Elders do not constitute a separate "class" of Christians, like the division between aristocrats and common folk, or between medieval priests and laypeople. Fundamentally, an elder is a Christian and a member of the church who has been set apart because his character is exemplary and he is able to teach.

The difference between an elder and a member, though formally designated by a title, is largely a difference of maturity, not class.

Like a parent with a child, the elder constantly works to call the member *up* and *into* maturity. It is a distinct office, to be sure. And not every mature Christian qualifies. Yet the point remains: an elder strives to duplicate himself insofar as he imitates Christ (see 1 Cor. 4:16; 11:1).

Speaking figuratively, he demonstrates how to use the hammer and saw, then places the tools into the member's hands. He plays the piano scale or swings the golf club, then asks the member to repeat what he has done.

To be a pastor/elder, you might say, makes one's whole life an exercise in show-and-tell. You remember show-and-tell. You would bring a toy to class, tell your classmates about it, and show it to them. You might let them handle it and see how it worked.

Such is a pastor or elder's life. He says to his church, "Let me teach you the way of the cross. Now watch me walk it. Here's how you endure suffering. Here's how you love your children. Here's how you share the gospel. Here's what generosity and justice look like. Let me show you how to be valiant for the truth and tender toward brokenness."

What is our job as members in relation to our elders? The author of Hebrews lays it out succinctly: "Remember your leaders, those who spoke to you the word of God. Consider the outcome of their way of life, and imitate their faith" (13:7).

Advantages of a Plurality

If the work of an elder is to lay down a way of life that every Christian can follow, churches benefit from having more than just one. We learn from watching the men in full-time vocational ministry, yes. Yet we also learn from the elder who works full-time as a teacher, at the factory, or in finance. Men in different vocations give us the opportunity to see how godliness might look in different spheres. Not only that, one pastor can do only so much shepherding work throughout the week. Two can do double the work. Three can triple it. And so forth.

The New Testament never tells us how many elders a church should have, but it consistently refers to the "elders" of a local church in the plural, as when Paul "sent to Ephesus and called the elders of the church" (Acts 20:17), or when James wrote, "Is anyone among you sick? Let him call for the elders of the church" (James 5:15; see also Acts 14:23; 16:4; 21:18; Titus 1:5).

Furthermore, there's no suggestion that every pastor or elder must be paid, and at least one passage suggests that only some would be (1 Tim. 5:17–18). It's also hard to imagine that churches in the first century could have paid all of their elders. Neither Collin nor I, for instance, receives income from a church. We work full-time for parachurch ministries. Yet both of us serve as elders or pastors in our respective congregations. We like to think of it as our evening and weekend job! Serving as "nonstaff" or "lay" elders (call it what you want) means we attend regular elder meetings, teach from time to time in different venues in the church's life, get called into various counseling or family-crisis situations, do premarital counseling, and more. It also means the church should always be near the forefront of our prayer lives, though we hope every other Christian aspires to do the same.

A plurality of elders does not mean that the pastor who preaches the most has no distinctive role. James was specially recognized as a leader in the church in Jerusalem (Act 15:13; 21:18), as was Timothy in Ephesus and Titus in Crete. In Corinth, Paul gave himself to preaching in a way not every lay elder would have (Acts 18:5; 1 Cor. 9:14; 1 Tim. 4:13; 5:17). Also, by being the regular voice who proclaims God's Word, a faithful preacher will probably find that a congregation begins to trust him in a unique way, such that even the other elders treat him as the first among equals and "especially" worthy of double honor—an income (1 Tim. 5:17). Still, the preacher or pastor is, fundamentally, just one more elder, formally equal with every other man called by the congregation.

A plurality of elders has a number of benefits:

- *It balances pastoral weakness.* No pastor has every gift. Other godly men will have complementary gifts, passions, and insights.
- *It adds pastoral wisdom.* None of us is omniscient.
- *It defuses an "us vs. him" mentality* that can sometimes arise between a church and the pastor.
- *It indigenizes leadership* in the congregation, so that, even if a staff pastor leaves, the congregation still possesses a solid bulwark of leadership.
- *It creates a clear discipleship trajectory* for the men in the church. Not every man will be called by God to serve as an elder. But every man should ask himself, *Why wouldn't I serve, and do what it takes to become the kind of man who serves the body in this way?* It's good to so aspire, Paul says (1 Tim. 3:1).
- *It also sets an example of discipleship for women.* Older women in the faith should give themselves to discipling the younger women, just as elders do for the whole congregation (Titus 2:3–4).

The Oil of Trust

Jesus's discipleship program, we said a moment ago, consists of elders doing their job of equipping members to do their job. What's crucial to recognize is that this works only when there is trust between members and elders. Trust is the oil that allows the engine of Jesus's discipleship program to operate. Without it, gears grind to a halt.

Think about it. We listen to, imitate, and follow the people we trust. If I believe you live with integrity, love me, and have my best interests in mind, it will be easier for me to receive your words of instruction or correction, even the tough stuff. If I don't trust these things about you, I'm going to second-guess and doubt everything you say, even the easy stuff. A healthy church, therefore, has leaders who are trustworthy but also people who are willing to trust.

Part of what made the COVID-19 quarantines so challenging is that trust naturally decreases when people don't see each other. Except in cases of conflict, physically being with people helps to create trust.

- "Yes, I know him. We had lunch. Good guy. I like him."
- "Well, the conversation just got worse and worse over email. Then we spoke in person and hammered it all out. Everything's better now."

Being together with people ordinarily grows trust, while absence tempts our hearts toward worry, skepticism, and even fear. Sure enough, many pastors learned during the COVID-19 quarantines that the congregational trust reserves they had spent years building up were quickly depleting. Things felt fine inside of churches for the first few weeks of quarantines in the spring of 2020. Then the pressure mounted as weeks turned into months. State governments tightened restrictions. Race protests then erupted throughout the United States in the summer. The American elections turned up the heat even more in the fall. And then questions over the presidential transition filled the winter. Exacerbating these political tensions was the fact that the churches were not gathering or were gathering only at partial capacity. A church that cannot gather and that has low reserves of trust is like a car with an engine that is running low on oil. As we said above, those gears will start to grind—between one member and elders and among members with each other, including through social media. At each step of the way, the political pressures working against unity grew stronger, while the challenges of gathering all together made trust among members and toward leaders even harder.

Both Collin and I spoke to dozens of pastors who were criticized by the political right, the political left, or both. They spoke of members—even long-standing leaders in their churches—leaving either for what they had said or had failed to say.

We cannot address the political issues here, but perhaps we can offer a quick pastoral word to any of you who have lost trust in your church leaders, whether for political or any other reasons. If that's you, this is a big deal. Your primary means of spiritual growth is hearing from God's Word. So if you, your spouse, or your children don't trust the pastors, you will have a hard time hearing God's Word from them week after week, which will hurt you spiritually over time. Therefore, this is a problem to address and resolve, if at all possible.

Maybe the problem is you. You need to at least consider this possibility, especially if you're turning against friends and other leaders you've known and trusted for years. Pray about it, and invite critique from someone you do trust. Maybe the problem is one or more of the elders, in which case you may need to address it directly with them.

We obviously cannot diagnose your specific situation here. But we can say that if all your efforts at restoring trust have failed, you may need to leave and find a church where you can trust the pastors enough that you'll allow them to challenge you when necessary. Don't just look for a church that will confirm everything you already know.

Yes, Christians should always work to reconcile. But sometimes humility requires us to place those more intractable conflicts on the shelf for a while and ask the Lord to solve them in his time and his way. Until that time comes, your continued ability to hear and apply God's Word without the stumbling block of broken trust remains crucial. Speaking as a pastor, I would rather someone leave my church because he doesn't trust me, even if I am convinced he is wrong and I am right, so that he can, over time, grow in godliness somewhere else. Maybe hearing God's Word preached somewhere else will allow him to grow so that, one day, we can reconcile. And probably I have some growing to do as well. It's more important for people to be under leadership they trust than to be under *my* leadership. The good news is, every gospel-preaching church is playing for the same kingdom team.

What about Deacons?

In addition to pastors/elders and members, the New Testament recognizes one other office: deacons. Deacons aren't a second body of decision makers, like some sort of bicameral legislature with the

House of Representatives counterbalancing the Senate. Rather, God gives deacons to do three things: spot and serve tangible needs, protect and promote church unity, and serve and support the ministry of the elders. Figuratively speaking, if the elders say, "Let's drive this car to Philadelphia," it's not the job of the deacons to come back and say, "No, let's go to Pittsburgh." Rather, they serve the elders and the whole church if they come back and say, "The engine in this car won't get us all the way to Philadelphia."

The story in Acts 6 never uses the noun *deacon*, but it uses the same word as a verb. Our Bible translates it as "serve." The backdrop is this: the church in Jerusalem was dividing along ethnic lines—as often seems to be the case in world history. The Greek-speaking widows were being neglected in the distribution of food in comparison to the Hebrew-speaking widows. The apostles observed that it would not serve the church for them to "deacon tables" (as the Greek literally reads, Acts 6:2) since they were called to give themselves to preaching the Word (or as they put it, "deaconing the Word," v. 4) and to prayer. Therefore, they instructed the church to find godly individuals who could do the work of making sure the widows were provided for. Caring for people's physical well-being embodies God's care; it often benefits them spiritually; and it acts as a witness to those outside the church.

Behind the physical care lies a second aspect of a deacon's work: striving for the unity of the body. By caring for the widows, the deacons helped make the food distribution among these women more equitable. This was important because *physical* neglect was causing *spiritual* disunity in the body (see Acts 6:1). The deacons were appointed to head off disunity in the church. Their job was to act as the shock absorbers for the body.

At a third level, the deacons were appointed to support the ministry of the apostles. By their ministry to widows, the deacons supported the teachers of the Word in their ministry. In this sense, deacons are fundamentally encouragers and supporters of the ministry of the elders. The result? "And the word of God continued to increase, and the number of the disciples multiplied greatly in Jerusalem" (Acts 6:7).

If every Christian is called to serve and work to maintain the unity of the church, why formally recognize an office of deacon? Because it reminds the church how close such service is to the heart of the gospel and our Lord Jesus Christ. He came not to be served, but to serve, he says. And the word he uses for "serve" is the word we translate as "deacon" (Mark 10:45). Jesus came "to deacon." Just as the elders provide an example of living by Christian doctrine, so deacons provide an example of living in service.

Praise God for the gifts of both elders and deacons. As you rediscover church, we hope that word sticks in your mind—*gifts*. God loves you, and he has given you these gifts: elders and deacons. Do you view them as gifts? Do you thank God for them as gifts? You can. They do what they do for your good and the advance of the gospel. God has given them a serious responsibility: "keeping watch over your souls, as those who will have to give an account" (Heb. 13:17). We can trust them to do this work—and obey them—when we trust that the God who knows and sees all things will hold them accountable.

Recommended Reading

Rinne, Jeramie. *Church Elders: How to Shepherd God's People Like Jesus*. Wheaton, IL: Crossway, 2014.

Smethurst, Matt. *Deacons: How They Serve and Strengthen the Church*. Wheaton, IL: Crossway, 2021.

Conclusion

You Don't Get the Church You Want,
but Something Better

WE WANT TO CONCLUDE this book with two stories. First, meet Todd and Allison. These are not their real names, and we've altered some details, but they are real people. Todd and Allison spent several years serving as missionaries in a large city in Asia with little church fellowship. Now they live in a large, heavily churched city in the American South, and they attend church weekly.

Sadly, their time on the mission field was tough on their marriage, and today they've developed a pattern of nonstop quarrelling. Ask Todd, and he'll say that Allison criticizes him incessantly. And, truth be told, he has begun to wonder if he can handle being married to this woman for the rest of his life. Allison feels the same way. Todd's easygoing charm, which makes everyone else smile, makes her stomach churn. Where is that charm when he comes home cranky, snaps at the kids, and questions what she has done with her day? She wonders why she married him.

Yet there is another problem behind all of this: they don't really have relationships with people in their church. They live on the periphery. They show up on Sunday for the seventy-five-minute service, but that's about it. No one knows they are struggling, and they never share their struggles.

Ironically, Todd and Allison think of themselves as mature Christians. They've both led Bible studies since their days in student leadership in Christian college groups. They know how to use the right lingo when praying in front of other people. Yet they are prouder than they realize. They don't recognize how much they need the church, and how Jesus means to care for them through their church. So they remain on the periphery, leaving the church unaware of their struggles and limited in the good it can do.

What do we want for Todd and Allison? We want them to humble themselves and push more deeply into the church, even if it means making sacrifices. They could look for ways to trim down their weekly schedules for the sake of building relationships. They could rethink their vacation and holiday plans, and look for ways to involve members in those plans. Frankly, they might even think about moving closer to the church so that frequent touch points are easier. Picking up that gallon of milk at the store and dropping it off at your fellow member's house easily becomes a thirty-minute conversation, something that rarely happens when you live thirty minutes away. Those unplanned conversations are not good for your schedule, but they just might be good for your soul.

Here's a second story, this one about Jazmine. Jazmine grew up with a stepfather who physically and sexually abused her, followed by a foster home where the same abuse occurred. By God's grace, she became a Christian as a young adult and married a Christian man. Yet the early years of marriage were difficult because of all the scars, fears, anger, and brokenness still packed deep inside her.

Wonderfully, God gave Jazmine a godly husband as well as a loving church. In the early years of marriage, the couple spent a lot of time in pastoral counseling. Jazmine also spent a lot of time with other women in the church. Every week they sat under the preaching of God's Word and in Bible study.

Little by little, Jazmine began to open up, like a timid flower warmed by the sun. She learned to trust. She gained control of her violent temper. She stopped viewing everyone in her life as a threat. She stopped viewing every minute of her days as a battle for control and self-protection. Even more, she began to turn outward and learned how to love and focus on other people. Where did they hurt? What burdens did they carry? How could she give herself to loving them? The non-Christian family members and friends who had known her as a child could only marvel.

What do we want for Jazmine? We want her to keep going. We want her to keep investing in others, even as she looks for others to invest in her.

You don't need to be an extrovert to be a faithful church member. Some people have a lot of emotional energy to spend, some only have a little. We're just saying, spend what you have. Be faithful with whatever resources God has given you to love and be loved by your church.

Don't Go Shopping

As we said at the start of the book, you have many reasons not to go to church. That's why we see this moment in history as an opportunity to rediscover church. The drift away from church didn't start with a pandemic or with partisanship. The world cultivates instincts in all of us that push against the vision of church you've encountered in this book. If churches are to thrive during whatever unknowns the future holds, they must be rediscovered.

The very language people use today to describe looking for a church suggests the fundamental problem. Folks talk about "shopping" for a church. When you're shopping for a church, you're asking what that church can do for you, not what you can do for the church. Shopping also suggests that church is a matter of mere preference, like choosing between brands of ketchup. And the customer is always right. Loyalty lasts only so long as the church continues to meet your needs.

Consider the role played by technology. We've already discussed how online video church and podcasts leave the impression that we don't need other ordinary Christians for our spiritual growth. If we can find our favorite worship music on YouTube and our favorite preacher on Spotify, then we can curate a personalized spiritual experience that surpasses whatever half-baked effort we can find down the street while jostling for space against frenzied families we don't care to know.

But the challenge new technologies pose to churches didn't begin just yesterday. We're not the first to observe that the automobile effectively ended church discipline for many churches. All of a sudden, someone could divorce his wife without cause and simply drive to a different neighborhood or town for church. He would never need to repent publicly at the demand of church leaders called to protect and care for his ex-wife and children. The point isn't that new technology is necessarily bad. It's just that it creates new challenges that we often overlook.

And so, again and again, the church needs to be rediscovered. This is because we're all prone to forget what God wants for us. The apostle Paul told the Philippians, "Do nothing from selfish ambition or conceit, but in humility count others more significant than yourselves. Let each of you look not only to his own interests, but also to the interests of others." In this he pointed to the example of Jesus, "who, though he was in the form of God, did not count equality with God a thing to be grasped, but emptied himself by taking the form of a servant, being born in the likeness of men" (Phil. 2:3–4, 6–7). Jesus humbled himself to die on the cross so that he could be exalted by God. If we want loving unity in the church, then we must follow the same path of self-denial. No other route will reach the summit, where we find God's approval: "Well done, good and faithful servant" (Matt. 25:21).

I (Collin) know a pastor who often says that no one gets the church they want. But everyone gets the church they need. We all need churches that call us to something greater than ourselves. We need churches that call us finally to God. When we follow the example of Jesus, we get the church we need.

Formative Institution

We're all trained today to leverage institutions such as family, work, and school to achieve our personal goals of attention and acceptance. Once we get what we want, or the institution asks us for something we don't want to give, we can discard it and move on to another target. Get a new job. Get a new family. Get a new school.

But personal growth doesn't usually work that way. Generally relationships don't change you for the better if they don't challenge you at your worst. Consider: Who are the most important people in your life? Do they only affirm you and every decision you make? Or do you trust that they will love you no matter what, and love you enough to tell you the truth? Relationships with family members and friends are forged through thick and thin. They will stand behind you at your best, stand next to you at your worst, and stand in front of you at your most vulnerable.

That's the kind of church we must rediscover. The church isn't just another institution we use to build a résumé and enhance our self-identity. The church forms us into men and women of God. We grow stronger together. At the same time, we learn more about who God intended us to be as individuals—our unique abilities and passions. The church doesn't erase our personalities. It enhances them by connecting us to the Creator who made us as we are and to others who call forth love and strength we never knew we had. You may not get the church you wanted. But you get the church you never knew you needed.

The two of us are not naive about how many churches fall short of this vision. You might think we underestimate the challenges. On the contrary, because of our positions, we know far more than most about the dark side of churches. We've experienced it ourselves. We've heard of it from others. We've seen it with friends and family members. And we're not asking you to tolerate abuse or heretical theology. We're not issuing a blanket endorsement for churches or condoning the misuse of power and authority that we know is common among churches, past and present.

We do, however, believe that you must expect friction in church. You should not expect to get along with everybody. You should not expect to share the same vision, the same priorities, the same strategies. Those moments of friction test all of us. They make us wonder if another church around the corner would be easier. It might, at least for a time, though probably not forever, because in that church you'll find sinners redeemed by grace. And you'll still be a sinner redeemed by grace. You'll find the good and the bad, maybe to a lesser degree. But no church this side of Jesus's return can avoid every disagreement and disappointment.

Think of church as something like waves rolling over rocks. The waves are the church. You and other church members are the rocks. Day after day, year after year, the waves flow without ceasing. They rush over each rock and jostle the rocks against one another. From month to month, you probably won't notice much difference. But over years, even decades, you'll observe the change. As the waves crash and the rocks tumble over one another, their rough edges become smooth. They take on a polished glint in the sun. No two rocks emerge from the process with the same size or shape. But in its own way, each becomes beautiful.

We shouldn't be surprised that Peter, the "rock" himself, picks up the imagery of stones to describe the church. First, Peter wants us to see that the church is built on the foundation of Jesus. He applies Isaiah 28:16 to Jesus: "Behold, I am laying in Zion a stone, / a cornerstone chosen and precious, / and whoever believes in him will not be put to shame" (1 Pet. 2:6).

Second, he wants us to realize that God didn't expect everyone to see Jesus as precious. For them, Peter cites Psalm 118:22 ("The stone that the builders rejected / has become the cornerstone") and Isaiah 8:14 ("A stone of stumbling / and a rock of offense") in 1 Peter 2:7–8.

Third, he wants us to see that Jesus has built something beautiful—us, the church: "As you come to him, a living stone rejected by men but in the sight of God chosen and precious, you yourselves like living stones are being built up as a spiritual house, to be a holy priesthood, to offer spiritual sacrifices acceptable to God through Jesus Christ" (1 Pet. 2:4–5).

You don't need to understand every Old Testament allusion here to marvel at what God has done in the church. As we believe in Jesus, we have been saved from our sin by God and for God. We have not been saved by ourselves and for ourselves. God is building something much bigger than any of us. Peter can hardly contain his excitement:

> But you are a chosen race, a royal priesthood, a holy nation, a people for his own possession, that you may proclaim the excellencies of him who called you out of darkness into his marvelous light. Once you were not a people, but now you are God's people; once you had not received mercy, but now you have received mercy. (1 Pet. 2:9–10)

That's a lot going on in your little ol' church when the sound system doesn't work, you're meeting in a parking deck because you're not safe from disease inside, the kids are whining for food, Sister Bethel snored through the benediction, Brother Jim posted something dumb on Facebook, and the pastor put in a C+ effort on sermon prep because he had a funeral and three unexpected hospital visits. When you rediscover church, you'll see the beauty where much of the world sees only rocks.

Just Show Up

We wrote this book to help you rediscover church, so that you could see why the body of Christ is essential. So what now? What's the next step? We have good news. It's easier than you could imagine. Just show up and ask how you can help.

That's right, that's the big takeaway from the book. When I (Collin) talk with new church members, I make a big promise. And so far, no one has ever returned to complain that I misled them. I promise that if they show up consistently (in our church, that means corporate worship on Sunday and home group on Wednesday) and seek to care for others, they will get everything they want out of the church. That could be spiritual growth, friendships, biblical knowledge, or practical help. They will get whatever they want from the church by fulfilling just those two simple tasks.

If you don't participate regularly, you don't get the formative experience of church. You don't grow in biblical knowledge through the teaching or in relational depth through praying with others. And if you don't seek the good of others, you learn to judge the church for how it fails to meet your needs and how others fail to reach out to you. Neither of us has ever seen people rediscover church and get what they want from the community unless they consistently show up and ask others how they can help.

Remember, you are the body of Christ. You might be a hand, an ear, or an eye. Whatever the appendage, you are essential.

The body doesn't function properly without you. And you need the body of Christ. So show up and ask around. Other Christians need you more than you can realize. One day you'll understand how much you needed them, too.

Acknowledgments

COLLIN WOULD LIKE TO THANK David Byers for his prayerful and tangible support while writing this book. Also, we gratefully acknowledge that small portions of the following articles and books have been adapted for this book with permission: *Chapter 2*: Jonathan Leeman, "The Corporate Component of Conversion," Feb. 29, 2012, 9Marks.org; *Chapter 3*: Jonathan Leeman, "Do Virtual Churches Actually Exist?" Nov. 9, 2020, 9Marks.org; Jonathan Leeman, "Churches: The Embassies and Geography of Heaven," Dec. 20, 2020, 9Marks.org; *Chapter 5*: Jonathan Leeman, "Church Membership Is an Office and a Job," May 7, 2019, 9Marks.org; *Chapter 6*: Jonathan Leeman, *Is It Loving to Practice Church Discipline?* (Wheaton, IL: Crossway, 2021); Jonathan Leeman, "The Great American Heartache: Why Romantic Love Collapses on Us," Nov. 21, 2018, DesiringGod.org; *Chapter 9*: Jonathan Leeman, "Church Membership Is an Office and a Job," May 7, 2019, 9Marks.org; Jonathan Leeman, *Understanding the Congregation's Authority* (Nashville: B&H, 2016).

General Index

Scripture Index

THE GOSPEL **COALITION**

The Gospel Coalition (TGC) supports the church in making disciples of all nations, by providing gospel-centered resources that are trusted and timely, winsome and wise.

Guided by a Council of more than 40 pastors in the Reformed tradition, TGC seeks to advance gospel-centered ministry for the next generation by producing content (including articles, podcasts, videos, courses, and books) and convening leaders (including conferences, virtual events, training, and regional chapters).

In all of this we want to help Christians around the world better grasp the gospel of Jesus Christ and apply it to all of life in the 21st century. We want to offer biblical truth in an era of great confusion. We want to offer gospel-centered hope for the searching.

Join us by visiting TGC.org so you can be equipped to love God with all your heart, soul, mind, and strength, and to love your neighbor as yourself.

TGC.org

 **9Marks**

Building Healthy Churches

9Marks exists to equip church leaders with a biblical vision and practical resources for displaying God's glory to the nations through healthy churches.

To that end, we want to see churches characterized by these nine marks of health:

1. Expositional Preaching
2. Gospel Doctrine
3. A Biblical Understanding of Conversion and Evangelism
4. Biblical Church Membership
5. Biblical Church Discipline
6. A Biblical Concern for Discipleship and Growth
7. Biblical Church Leadership
8. A Biblical Understanding of the Practice of Prayer
9. A Biblical Understanding and Practice of Missions

Find all our Crossway titles and other resources at 9Marks.org.